STREET SMARTS

STREET SMARTS

ADVENTURES ON THE ROAD
AND IN THE MARKETS

Jim Rogers

CROWN
BUSINESS
New York

2014 Crown Business International Edition

Published in the United States by Crown Business,
an imprint of the Crown Publishing Group,
a division of Random House LLC,
a Penguin Random House Company, New York.
www.crownpublishing.com

CROWN BUSINESS is a trademark and CROWN and the Rising Sun
colophon are registered trademarks of Random House LLC.

Originally published in hardcover in the United States by Crown Business,
an imprint of the Crown Publishing Group,
a division of Random House LLC, New York, in 2013.

Crown Business books are available at special discounts for bulk purchases
for sales promotions or corporate use. Special editions, including
personalized covers, excerpts of existing books, or books with corporate
logos, can be created in large quantities for special needs. For more
information, contact internationalsales@randomhouse.com.

Library of Congress Cataloging-in-Publication Data
Rogers, Jim, 1942–
Street smarts / Jim Rogers.
p. cm.
Includes index.
1. Investments. 2. Investment analysis.
3. Portfolio management. I. Title.
HG4521.R686 2013
332.6—dc23 2012027063

ISBN 978-0-553-41871-2
eBook ISBN 978-0-307-98609-2

Printed in the United States of America

Book design by Jaclyn Reyes
Cover design by Jessie Sayward Bright
Cover photography by Danny Santos II

10 9 8 7 6 5 4 3

To Baby Bee
May You Enjoy More Adventures
Than Your Daddy
and Be Twice as Smart

I met a traveller from an antique land

Who said: Two vast and trunkless legs of stone

Stand in the desert. Near them, on the sand,

Half sunk, a shattered visage lies, whose frown,

And wrinkled lip, and sneer of cold command,

Tell that its sculptor well those passions read

Which yet survive, stamped on these lifeless

    things,

The hand that mocked them and the heart that fed:

And on the pedestal these words appear:

"My name is Ozymandias, king of kings:

Look on my works, ye Mighty, and despair!"

Nothing beside remains. Round the decay

Of that colossal wreck, boundless and bare

The lone and level sands stretch far away.

        —"Ozymandias," Percy Bysshe Shelley

CONTENTS

STREET
SMARTS

1

PORTRAIT OF THE INVESTOR
AS A YOUNG MAN

My hometown, Demopolis, sits in the heart of the Alabama Cane-brake, where the Black Warrior and the Tombigbee Rivers meet. The largest city in Marengo County, it lies in the center of a region of Georgia, Alabama, and Mississippi known historically as the Black Belt, so named for the layer of naturally rich, thick black prairie soil that almost two hundred years ago nourished the growth of vast cotton plantations, some of which outlasted slavery, none of which survived the boll weevil.

It was in that soil, when I was a boy, that my friends and I would dig for bait before setting off to spend the day fishing. Channel catfish are omnivorous and will strike at just about anything they can smell—they are able to smell just about everything—and earthworms, on a hot summer day, are a lot easier to gather than crickets. I must have been eight years old and we were digging in the backyard of my house when my cousin Wade, who was about ten months older than I, ventured a remark that, while entirely incomprehensible at the time, remains vivid to me to this day.

"If we keep digging," he said, "we'll end up in China."

I was not ignorant of the fact that the world was round, but not until I was able to consult a globe—I was an enthusiastic researcher even then—did I come to appreciate that directly opposite Alabama, on the other side of the planet, sprawled the vast landmass of the People's Republic, where covered in dirt and drenched with sweat I would eventually emerge if I were energetic enough to keep digging.

Decades have intervened since then, and I have followed a more circuitous route, but on the very doorstep of China is where I find myself living today, the father of two little blue-eyed blondes who speak Mandarin as fluently as they speak English.

How I came to be a permanent resident of Singapore is a story about digging of a different kind, excavation perhaps less arduous, though no less energetic. It is a result of my endless effort to experience firsthand the inner workings of the world, to get out and unearth the real story, to explore it all for myself.

I have circumnavigated the globe twice now, once by motorcycle, once by car, investigating the world at ground level, charting the shifting circumstances of more than a hundred nations in the course of those five years. For me, understanding history and its consequences has not been an armchair endeavor, but a hands-on adventure. It has led to great personal and material rewards, and it inevitably led me here, far from the backwoods of

Alabama, to this largely Chinese outpost on the southern tip of the Malay Peninsula.

If history affirms anything, it is the proposition put forth by the Greeks that "nothing endures but change." It originated with the philosopher Heraclitus in the sixth century B.C., when he informed us aphoristically that it is not possible to step twice into the same river. Success in life is measured by the ability to anticipate change, and I came to Singapore in response to the realization that the world is in the midst of a historic shift, a dramatic reshaping of the terrain, a decline of US leadership in the world and a commensurate rise in Asia.

I write this in the midst of a global financial crisis that most of the world's politicians would have you believe is temporary. Things, we are told, will turn around. I will not argue with that. I am here to tell you, simply, that things are unlikely to turn around permanently in your lifetime. The staggering debt loads in many countries will lead to major changes in the way we all live and work. Many old institutions, traditions, political parties, governments, cultures, even nations will decline or collapse or simply disappear, just as has always happened in times of political and economic turmoil.

The investment bank Bear Stearns, for instance, was decades old when it went under in 2008. The financial-services firm Lehman Brothers, when it foundered that same year, had been in business for more than a century and a half. The cave-in of those long-established, global corporations exemplifies the changing circumstances faced by many American institutions. Harvard, Princeton, and Stanford, though they might not know it yet, may be heading toward bankruptcy. Museums, hospitals, and other institutions we know and love are headed for trouble, and we are going to see a lot of them vanish in the upheaval, be it financial or economic.

Some have labeled me an alarmist, a modern-day Cassandra. But nothing I see in the future need serve as cause for alarm, or even come as a surprise. The winds of change are blowing, they are blowing from the direction of China, and they are blowing in predictable fashion. What we are witnessing is business as usual, history turning a familiar page. And throughout history such moments of transition have presented opportunities to the attentive, so I am wildly optimistic about many things to come.

If you were smart at the start of the nineteenth century, you made your way to London. If you were smart at the start of the twentieth, you packed up and moved to New York. If you are smart at the start of the twenty-first, you will find your way to Asia. A hundred years from now, the cycle of change could lead anywhere—at the end of the first millennium, all the smart people moved to Córdoba, the flower of Islamic Spain, at the time the intellectual center of Europe and the most populous city in the world.

I moved to Asia in 2007, and even more significantly, I moved my children here. In their lifetime, a knowledge of Asia will be indispensable to success, and a mastery of Mandarin will prove, throughout the world, as important as the mastery of English does today. Power and influence in the world moved from Great Britain to the United States in the 1920s and 1930s. The loss of British leadership was exacerbated by a financial crisis and political mismanagement, and it was unnoticed by many until twenty or thirty years later. Power and influence are now moving from

the United States to Asia, a loss of American leadership acceler-
ated by the same forces, and a change that likewise remains unnoticed by most.

The transition to Asia comes at a time of a second historical shift. In the depths of a financial meltdown, the world is on
the verge of a transition away from finance itself, a cyclical shift
away from financial firms as a source of prosperity. Throughout
history there have been periods where financiers were in charge,
and there have been periods where the producers of real goods—
farmers, miners, energy providers, lumberjacks—were in charge.
In the '50s, '60s, and '70s, before the big bull market, Wall Street
and the City of London were backwaters. They will be again. The
money shufflers are in decline, and those identified in the book
of Joshua as the "hewers of wood and drawers of water" will now
inherit the earth.

Examining the forces of history responsible for the changes
in question, embracing the simple hypothesis that nothing goes
on forever, I have come to appreciate the observation of another of
civilization's great thinkers, Albert Einstein, who said: "Only two
things are infinite: the universe and human stupidity. And I'm not
so sure about the former."

Let us not forget that Cassandra, the Trojan princess who
made a nuisance of herself when she warned against dragging
the Greeks' wooden horse into the city, if remembered for no
other attribute, is remembered for having been right.

My aim in writing this book, among other things, is to cast
light on how we came to be where we are and how individuals can
go about educating themselves to prepare for the future. In doing

so, I will share with you insights gained over the course of a lifetime in finance, investing, and the pursuit of adventure, lessons I learned growing up, following a road that led from the soil of the Black Belt to this Southeast Asian city-state on the other side of the globe, a lifelong journey in the course of which I made the whole world my backyard.

MY ADVENTURE IN THE MARKETS began in the spring of 1964. I was a senior at Yale, and I found myself headed to Wall Street in much the same way that I had earlier found myself headed to the Ivy League: I stumbled into it.

In high school, I was an enthusiastic member of the Key Club, a student-led service organization, part of Kiwanis International, which until 1976 was restricted to boys. Membership in the Demopolis Key Club was something of a big deal because the local sponsor had made the decision to admit only five boys a year. The year I served as president, the Demopolis club won the award as the world's best Key Club from a small town. Every year, back then, Yale University granted a four-year scholarship to a member of Key Club International. The scholarship was how I heard of Yale. Had it not been for the Key Club I never would have applied.

The school I fully expected to attend, the only college other than Yale to which I applied, was the University of the South in Sewanee, Tennessee, a liberal arts college affiliated with the Episcopal Church. I was accepted at Sewanee shortly after sending in my application. It was not until April or May, some considerable time after my father sent Sewanee the required $50 acceptance fee, that I received a thick envelope from Yale containing notification that I had been accepted there and had been awarded the Key Club scholarship of $2,000 a year.

I was astonished.

I was seventeen and knew little about Yale except that it was in New Haven, Connecticut. My parents, however, were experienced enough to appreciate the significance of my being accepted. Both were college graduates. They had met at the University of Oklahoma, where both were Phi Beta Kappa. My father had studied petroleum engineering, my mother liberal arts. To them, my attending Yale was pretty big stuff. "We are a little bit worried to have you setting off to that bastion of liberalism in the North," I remember my father saying, but in fact both he and my mother were ecstatic. My father's joy would be tempered somewhat by his subsequent failure to get back the $50 he had sent to Sewanee. Fifty dollars in 1960 in Demopolis was a lot of money, and is still a lot of money today, but back then it was worth about seven times as much as it is worth currently.

I was the eldest of five brothers and one of fewer than fifty students in my high school class, and I was quick to exhibit to all of them the exaggerated sense of my own importance that flowed from my good fortune. I immediately started putting on the big dog, as we say in those parts, but my inflated sense of myself was destined to be short-lived. Slowly it dawned on me, *Oh, oh, now I have to go to Yale*. And I was suddenly scared, because I knew I was in way over my head. I wondered, *What am I going to do now?*

That summer, traveling to attend the Key Club convention in Boston, I got off the train in New Haven and went to the Yale admissions office. I wanted to know why I had been accepted. I hoped that by asking that question, I might get an idea of what to expect and understand what might be expected of me. The admissions director pulled out my folder and said, "What do you mean? Look, you graduated first in your class. You got a hundred in many of your subjects. Your *average* was almost a hundred."

Yeah, but that was in Demopolis. Oh, my gosh, I thought, *these guys think I'm smart, they think I know something.*

Feeling totally unprepared to compete with students from prestigious northeastern prep schools, I arrived at Yale ready to study that much harder than everyone else. A test came up, I remember, and one of my classmates said that he was going to study five hours to prepare for it. "This test," he said, "is worth five hours of study." I found his reasoning very peculiar. My approach was to study as much as was necessary until I knew the subject, and then study some more just to be sure. It was the approach I took to everything, a discipline my brothers and I picked up from my parents: There is no such thing as enough. You just keep studying, or keep working, or keep researching, whatever the task happens to be.

Today, I wish I knew how to instill this characteristic in my children. I wish I could call my father or mother and say, "What pill did you give us?" Call it discipline, call it diligence, call it work ethic—we all have it, my brothers and I. I do not know where it comes from. I wish I could find the gene. I am certainly not alone in recognizing the value of persistence—we all know smart people who are not successful; we all know talented people who are not successful. Persistence is what makes the difference.

The cost of tuition and room and board at Yale back then was $2,300. With my $2,000 scholarship I was $300 short to start with, and that was before the cost of books and other routine expenses. I got a job as a busboy in the dining hall a few hours a week and continued taking part-time jobs at the university all the time I was there.

Work experience in one's youth offers quantifiable benefits. While teaching the value of money, it also helps you develop an identity; in learning to manage finances, you gain a tangible measure of autonomy. I started paying my own way early in life, well before arriving at Yale. My father, when I was six, teaching me that "money does not grow on trees," insisted that I pay for my own baseball glove. I went down to Braswell Hardware in Demopolis and picked out a glove that cost four dollars. I took it home, and every Saturday I returned to pay the proprietor, Cruse Braswell, fifteen cents until the full price had been paid. Years later, a Columbia business school dean, citing a university study, told me that the single most important predictor of a happy life in adulthood was having a paying job as a teenager.

All in all, I had a fine time at Yale. I majored in history and competed as a coxswain on the crew, lettering in my sophomore and junior years (I did not cox as a senior). I even did a little acting and landed a couple of leading roles. One was directed by John Badham, class of 1961. Can you imagine what a hit his movie *Saturday Night Fever* would have been if he had remembered me for the lead! But as much as I loved it, I never went too far with it, for the same reason that I did not cox as a senior. I devoted the time to my studies instead. And the discipline paid off. Not as smart as everybody else, I managed to graduate cum laude.

And like many people when they graduate from college, I had absolutely no idea what I was going to do next.

I was accepted at Harvard Business School and at both Harvard and Yale law schools, but I might just as well have applied to medical school for all the enthusiasm I had for choosing among them. What I really wanted to do was travel. As a boy I had loved reading Dickens's *The Pickwick Papers*, and the gentlemen of the Pickwick Club and their picaresque adventures may have played some part in the development of my wanderlust. I was self-aware enough, even at twenty-one, to realize that just going away—in my case, from rural Alabama to a fancy Connecticut Ivy League school located a thousand miles from home—had been a significant part of my education. It was an eye-opener. It taught me a lot.

"And what should they know of England who only England know?" as Rudyard Kipling wrote in "The English Flag."

I always felt very inadequate around a lot of the guys at Yale, because many of them had traveled abroad. My passion had always been to know and see more of the world. I remember, some years earlier, expressing that longing to my then girlfriend, Janet Corley. "I'm sixteen years old," I lamented, "and I have really never been anywhere." The worldly Janet could only sympathize. "I'm sixteen, and I've been a lot of places," she pointed out. "I've been to Birmingham, I've been to Mobile, I've been to Montgomery, Tuscaloosa . . ."

Out of the urge to broaden my horizons, I applied for various scholarships to study overseas. By the time recruiters showed up on campus I had received an academic scholarship, granted by Yale, to read Philosophy, Politics and Economics (PPE) at Balliol College, Oxford. It was my opportunity to travel abroad, and it provided the ancillary benefit of an additional two years in which I could put off deciding what to do with my life. (And secretly, I harbored the fanciful notion of coxing the legendary Oxford and Cambridge Boat Race.) I was eager to set forth. All I needed was a summer job.

Dominick & Dominick Inc., one of the oldest privately held investment firms in the United States, recruited heavily at Yale. A white-shoe, blue-blooded, Yale-slash-Ivy-League outfit, it was one of several companies with which I scheduled interviews when recruiters set up on campus. I had little success with the other companies, but I got on famously with the Dominick & Dominick recruiter, Joe Cacciotti. He was a kid who had grown up on the streets of the Bronx and somehow had made it to Harvard; I was a kid who had grown up in the backwoods of Alabama and some-how had made it to Yale. We seemed to have a lot in common—with one glaring exception. Dominick & Dominick was looking for full-time employees.

"I can't take a full-time job with you," I told him, "but I'd love to come work for you for the summer."

Founded in 1870, one of the earlier members of the New York Stock Exchange, Dominick & Dominick was not in the habit of setting up shop at Yale every spring to take on summer help. For some reason—based, I have to assume, on Joe's endorsement—the company made an exception in my case, and in the summer of 1964, I went to work on Wall Street.

By the time I left for Oxford later that year, I knew exactly what I wanted to do for the rest of my life.

UNTIL I WENT to work there, all I knew about Wall Street was that it was somewhere in New York and that something bad had happened there in 1929. I did not know there was a difference between stocks and bonds, much less what the difference was. I knew nothing of currencies or commodities. I doubt if I knew that the price of copper went up and down in the markets.

That first summer at Dominick & Dominick I worked in the research department, answering wires from brokers: Does General Motors pay a dividend and if so, how much? I thrived on digging up information. I also worked on the trading desk, where they did what was known as "making a market" in various stocks that were not listed on the New York Stock Exchange—buying and selling stocks that were traded over the counter in the days before NASDAQ. I learned a lot about how the markets actually worked on a transaction basis.

I remember the firm's senior partner asking me where I had gone to school. I answered that I had attended Yale. "Good, because we do not want too many redbellies or tiger boys here," he said, referring to Harvard and Princeton grads, respectively. Meeting him, I took the opportunity to ask his advice about going to business school. He said, "They will teach you nothing useful there. Come down here and sell soybeans short, once, and you will learn much more about markets than you will wasting two years with them."

It was a very exciting summer. I saw the world in a way I had never seen it before. All of a sudden my studies of history and current events were more than theoretical exercises—they had practical value. My passion to know the world was put to a purpose. As a student of history, I found it fascinating to learn how the markets were driven by world events. But what really struck home, for the first time in my life, was how predictably, throughout history, world events were driven by the markets.

I learned that everything was connected. I learned that a revolution in Chile was going to affect the price of copper, and thus the price of electricity and the price of houses—the price of everything—all over the world, having an impact on everyone, including homeowners in Toledo. I learned, also, that if you could figure out that a revolution in Chile was coming, you could earn a pretty good living.

What I discovered that summer was my future. Wall Street was a place where people would actually pay me to exercise my inclination to explore. And they would pay me a lot if I did it right. On Wall Street I would be compensated for doing all the things I loved to do. It was the first of two summers at Dominick & Dominick, and I knew instantly that, after Oxford, I was not going to attend law school. I was not going to attend business school. I was going to go back and work on Wall Street as soon as I could.

2

INNOCENT ABROAD

Philosophy, Politics and Economics, as an academic degree, was designed in the 1920s at Oxford, specifically at Balliol College, as a modern alternative to Classics, to prepare those who were entering the British civil service to administer the empire. Little, of course, did the British know at the time that the empire was on its last legs. I now know enough about university education to wonder whether sending out a lot of self-important PPE graduates might not have actually hastened the empire's decline.

The United Kingdom in 1918 was the richest, most powerful country in the world. If you looked at a map of the world, you saw nothing but red. The British Empire was everywhere. The nineteenth century had been a century of great world trade; it saw the integration of world economies—economies were opening up everywhere—largely to the benefit of the British, a maritime power. It was an exciting time economically, socially, and artistically.

But empires always overreach. They always overspend. And by 1918, the British Empire was already corroding from within. The blood and treasure invested in the Boer War had led to the same kind of internal turmoil and debt that would be engendered a century later by the vain politicians of a subsequent empire, the United States, who casually threw away lives and resources on wasted efforts in Vietnam and Iraq, overextending the nation in every way: militarily, geopolitically, economically, not to mention morally.

The First World War, a political reaction to a horrible act of terrorism, had advanced Britain's overextension. Members of the British and German royal houses, as recently as 1910, had been vacationing together, the fastest of friends (and relatives). By 1914, their children were slaughtering each other in the trenches of France. Britain went into the First World War overextended and came out of it even worse, with huge international debts. By 1939, it blocked the mighty pound sterling—making it extremely difficult to take the currency out of the country—and imposed exchange controls that lasted forty years. The country was no longer competitive. In the aftermath of the Second World War came a gradual drawdown of its military presence beyond Europe. By the 1960s, it could no longer defend imperial interests "east of Suez," much less maintain an empire.

One of those interests was Singapore. Singapore's title, the Lion City, is a direct translation of the original Sanskrit, *singh* (lion) and *pura* (city), and derives from the city's foundation legend as recounted in the *Malay Annals*. Upon coming ashore to explore the island, Sang Nila Utama, a Palembang prince, is said to have sighted what he was told was a lion, and seeing it as a good omen, he took its name for the kingdom he founded there early in the fourteenth century. (What he sighted, if he sighted anything, was more likely a Malayan tiger, for lions, even Asiatic lions, have never ranged east of the Indian subcontinent. Tigers still roamed wild in Singapore as recently as the 1930s.) The British took possession of the Lion City in 1824.

In 1969, on the eve of the British withdrawal from the island, colonial officers, swilling their farewell drinks at Raffles, could be heard muttering, "This is the end of Singapore." All agreed it was going to hell, a swamp, desperately poor, an outpost of half a million people with no hope of improvement. Returning home to ride out the waning days of the empire, those same civil servants could only gape from afar at the unfolding of what is perhaps the greatest success story of the past forty years. Singapore today is one of the richest countries in the world, and perhaps per capita *the* richest in the world, based on international currency reserves.

It was Britain that went to hell. In 1976, unable to sell government bonds, the erstwhile superpower suffered the indignity of seeking an International Monetary Fund bailout. After overseeing an empire in 1918 on which the sun never set, the country descended into economic chaos within a single generation and was bankrupt within three.

By the time Britain recovered, the United States had been throwing its weight around for the better part of half a century as the world's dominant power, economically, militarily, and geopolitically. Margaret Thatcher, elected in 1979, takes credit for the eventual British turnaround. And she is responsible for many positive changes. But the fact is that 1979 was also the year that North Sea oil started flowing. You find me an elephant oil field and I will show you a very good time, too.

Along with the fiscal discipline she necessarily imposed, Margaret Thatcher put an end to exchange controls, which had been in effect in Britain since 1939. When I arrived at Oxford in 1964, sterling was not a freely convertible currency. You could not buy the pound sterling or sell it, except in accord with strict controls and regulations. You could not take significant amounts of the currency out of the country. The pound was in constant crisis. Every week in my economics tutorials, consideration eventually turned to the latest problem with the pound. The rate was set at $2.80, but that was clearly too high. It did not accurately reflect the health—the ill health—of the British economy. The country was on the verge of bankruptcy, growing less competitive in every way. No one would invest in Britain, and the British could not invest elsewhere.

As an Oxford student, I had a foreigner's bank account. It was noted in the account that the money I deposited was foreign money, dollars in my case, and I could therefore take it in and out as I pleased. The bank kept a record of how much foreign currency I brought in. I would not be allowed to leave the country with more money than that. The account was very strictly and rigidly controlled. I did not have much money to begin with, but I was careful never to take more than a certain amount out of the bank over any given weekend, because I was always certain that it would be the weekend when the government devalued the currency. Even to a naive twenty-two-year-old, it was clear that something had to give. For two years I walked around with never more than two-and-six in my pocket—two shillings six pence, a British half crown.

As the situation got worse and worse—as the balance of trade grew worse and the nation's debts increased—I was eventually proved right. But the government did not devalue until the year after I left. I was right, but my timing was wrong: this particular trait—accurate but early—would come to repeat itself throughout my career as an investor, a mixed blessing that would be one of its more prominent features. The pound was devalued to $2.40, but the rate did not hold. With the advent of floating exchange rates in the 1970s, it fell to a low of $1.06. If the currency had been able to undergo gradual adjustments over that period, British industries might have adapted, adjusting to potential changes and staying more competitive. Instead the currency collapsed.

Under Thatcher, the City of London became an international financial center once again, and Britain has since had a great twenty or twenty-five years. But the North Sea oil is now drying up. The United Kingdom, once again, is a net importer of oil. And with the world shifting away from finance as a driver of prosperity—finance is going to be a terrible place to make money for the next twenty or thirty years—the City of London is drying up too. The country is suffering under staggering debts and is once more in decline.

IN 2010, I had occasion to revisit Oxford with my family. I was invited to deliver one of the Oliver Smithies lectures at Balliol

College, a lecture series named for and funded by the British-born American geneticist and 2007 Nobel laureate in medicine who was educated at Balliol. I had been asked to share my outlook on the future with today's Oxford students. But if you were to ask my daughters the purpose of our visit, the answer would be: "to give them a boat."

Let me give you some background.

At Oxford there is really only one sport of consequence: rowing. And there is no rowing event of greater consequence than what is referred to simply as The Boat Race.

The Oxford and Cambridge Boat Race was first held in 1829. It is rowed between competing eights every spring on the river Thames, on the last Saturday in March or the first Saturday in April. Having coxed three years at Yale, I had read about and heard about The Boat Race, and I was well aware of its significance when I arrived at Oxford. Competing in it makes you something of a national hero in the United Kingdom. Flash that credential alone, and few are the pubs anywhere in England where you will not find a patron eager to buy you a pint, or—because it is England, after all—several.

(In 2010, some 250,000 spectators lined the four-and-a-half-mile course to watch The Boat Race, which attracted more than six million television viewers in the United Kingdom alone. It was live-streamed or broadcast by the BBC in over 150 countries.)

Hundreds of students from the crews of the various colleges at Oxford, including a lot of coxes, compete each spring for the nine slots available on what is known as the Blue Boat. Blue refers to the University Sporting Blue, the honor that is won by athletes at Oxford and Cambridge who compete at the highest level in certain sports, and that, by definition, is earned by the members of both Boat Race crews, all of whom are known as "blues"—dark blue at Oxford, light blue at Cambridge.

When I was selected to cox the Blue Boat in my second year at Oxford, I became only the second American to do so in the 137 years since The Boat Race was first held. As it happened, the first American to do so had also attended both Yale and Balliol. And the year that he coxed—I think it was 1951—the Oxford boat sank. When it was announced that Oxford had decided on this guy Rogers, a graduate of Yale who was at Balliol College, a great hoopla went up: "Oh, my God, here's another one that's going to sink Oxford."

I almost lost my place in the boat. Once you are selected you have to buy your blue blazer, special blue scarves, and special sweaters, along with white trousers, and the entire outfit is to be worn with black shoes. I did not have any black shoes. I owned only one pair of dress shoes, and they were cordovan, which I had bought as a compromise between black and brown. I could not afford both, and I decided that the dark brown, the cordovan, could go both ways. I remember the president of the Oxford University Boat Club, Duncan Clegg, coming to me and telling me, "You have got to get rid of those brown shoes."

I said, "They're not brown, they are *dark* brown, they're cordovan."

And, for me, they were very expensive.

"No," he said, "it won't do."

I said, "I just don't have the money. It has cost me a fortune to buy all the things I've had to buy so far, and I just can't afford to buy another pair of shoes. And if that means losing my position in the boat, there is nothing I can do."

In the end they let me wear my brown shoes.

That year, 1966, we beat Cambridge in The Boat Race by three and a quarter lengths.

The year before, in 1965, for the first time in the history of the race (establishing a tradition that continues today), the reserve crews of the two universities faced off in a preliminary competition. I coxed the Isis boat for Oxford. (The reserve crew boat is named for a stretch of the river Thames, the Isis, which flows through the city.) That year, my first year at Oxford, I had been in contention for a spot in the Blue Boat. But thanks to a certain "unpleasantness," as the British might say, I almost quit rowing altogether.

Since all sport at Oxbridge was completely nonprofessional (we were even required to buy our own uniforms), the rowing coaches at Oxford were all volunteers, and that year the finishing coach, who would oversee the crew of The Boat Race, was an Australian named Sam Mackenzie, a former world champion sculler. Something of a hustler, always on the make, Sam had been a professional chicken sexer by occupation and had been highly regarded in the poultry industry for his exceptional skill. In picking who would race against Cambridge, Mackenzie and the president of the boat club, a student oarsman named Miles Morland that year, would make the final decision.

Christopher Dodd recounted the problem I ran into in his 1983 book, *The Oxford and Cambridge Boat Race*:

"Jim Rogers Jr was a happy man at Balliol College and steering Isis until he received a letter [from his father] in January which both shocked and confused him. He sat on it for several days, finding himself an innocent abroad. He then decided that because of what it said his easiest course was to resign from the whole scene. He did not want to be involved in a game where he had no idea who was playing with a full deck and who wasn't. He went to his coach David Hardy and told him that he wanted to give up his seat in the Isis crew, that he wouldn't go on. Hardy smelled a rat and followed it. He called on Rogers and tried to get out of him why he had quit. It didn't make sense to Hardy. Rogers had been doing a good job. So Rogers showed him his letter. . . .

"[It had been] sent to Jim Rogers Sr in Alabama [who] hardly knew where Oxford was or what the Boat Race was all about, but he understood the tenor of Mackenzie's remarks. The letter contained two or three paragraphs of chitchat about Oxford, the Boat Race, and how the man's son was getting on. At the bottom was a hand-written note to the effect that if there was a large increase in Mackenzie's bank account, a sum of four figures being suggested, then Rogers Jr was assured of a place in the blue boat. On the very bottom Rogers Sr had written [to his son]: 'Is this man crazy, or am I?'"

I had been at Oxford only a few months. Other members of the crew had known one another for years. I had no idea what was going on but knew that whatever was happening, it was something I did not want to be involved in, and the only solution I saw to the dilemma was simply to walk away. It seemed the path of least resistance. Hardy talked me out of quitting. He took the letter to the boat club's faculty adviser and treasurer, a law don named Vere Davidge, the bursar of Keble College, an oarsman himself. Over his ever-present decanter of port, he told me, "Sam was never really our kind," and Mackenzie was eventually fired.

The eight Isis oarsmen and I were victorious in the race against Cambridge, and we decided to remain together so that we could compete that summer at the Henley Royal Regatta.

A major social event in the United Kingdom, the regatta takes place over five days in July and is called royal because its patron is a member of the Royal Family: Prince Philip in those days. Crews come from all over the world to race at Henley. It is one of the pinnacles of the sport. If your university crew does well, rowing at Henley is your reward. I had heard of the regatta at Yale, and knew all about it. In fact, I was steeped in the lore of it. But it never occurred to me that I might go there someday and compete. The most prestigious event is the Grand Challenge Cup for Men's Eights, which has been awarded since the regatta was first staged in 1839. My oarsmen and I decided to compete for the Thames Cup, which in 1965, as it is today, was the number two cup for eights. Excited enough just to be there, I was thrilled when we won, setting a record for the Thames Cup on our way to winning the gold medal, my first entry into the *Guinness Book of Records*.

Today the Balliol College Boat Club has both men's and women's crews, and their first boats for eights are named the *Beeland Rogers* and the *Happy Rogers*, respectively. I donated the *Happy Rogers*, named for my elder daughter, to the women's crew in 2007. The *Beeland Rogers*, named for my second daughter, I donated to the men's crew shortly thereafter. The men's boat arrived in 2009 in time for Eights Week at Oxford, also known as Summer Eights, the culmination of the rowing season. After The Boat Race, it was the university's most important rowing event, and a great social occasion as well, a four-day regatta of races, with seven men's divisions and six for women, featuring 158 boats. Some colleges enter as many as five crews each for men and women. In 2008, the Balliol Men's 1st VIII had placed Head of the River for the first time in fifty-two years. In 2010, in the *Happy Rogers*, the Balliol Women's 1st VIII placed Head of the River for the first time in their thirty-year history. (They repeated in 2011.) The men rowed Head again in 2009 before being bumped down, but both my girls had boats that rowed Head of the River.

The Headship dinner celebrating the women's victory in 2010 coincided with the Smithies lecture I delivered that year, and my wife, Paige, and I attended the celebration with the children. Happy, aged seven at the time, and Baby Bee, aged two and a half, both outfitted in their finest dresses, had the opportunity to officially christen their boats with champagne. I awarded each member of the women's crew a 2010 gold sovereign and each member of the men's crew a similar coin dated 2008, commemorating the year of their victory, which Happy handed out. And then she announced that she would be donating a second boat to the women, called the *Happy Rogers II*.

NOT SURPRISINGLY, my remarks confounded the assembled Balliol students. Their bewilderment was understandable. They knew as well as I how much things had changed since I had studied at Oxford. What they did not appreciate was that the things that had changed—especially the rise of finance—were now changing back again.

In my second year at Oxford, my economics don, Professor Wilfred Beckerman, had said to me, "We don't have anybody like you here. We don't know what to do with you. Most people here could not care less about the stock market. As far as we're concerned the City of London is insignificant. It has little to do with the world economy, let alone the economy of the United Kingdom. Nobody cares."

In the 1960s, most of the professors at Balliol were socialists. The free market meant nothing to the academics who were advising the government. When I arrived at Oxford in 1964, London's financial district, the City of London, was all but ignored. The best and the brightest students at Balliol were seeking careers in government service and academia. A job in the City was for the idiot sons.

My economics tutor was right. The City had become a backwater, as had Wall Street.

By the time I returned to lecture in 2010, times had obviously changed. London was again a global financial center, indeed the leading center of finance in the world. And the Balliol students attending my lecture belonged to a generation of scholars who aspired to careers in investment banking. Given their way, many of them would have been running hedge funds out of their dorm rooms.

They wanted to do what I did, they told me, and asked me what they should be studying. Study philosophy, I said, study history. No, no, no, they said, they wanted to work in the City; they wanted to be rich. If that were the case, I answered, they should stay away from the City, because it would soon be a backwater again. Finance is over, I told them. Study agriculture instead. If they wanted to be rich, I advised, they should all become farmers.

Today, the United States, alone, graduates over two hundred thousand MBAs a year, as opposed to five thousand annually in 1958. The rest of the world produces tens of thousands more (there were *none* abroad in 1958). Over the next few decades, those business degrees will be worthless, a waste of both time and money. There is now huge debt in the financial community, which is a change from previous decades. There are new controls, regulations, and taxes that will make finance more expensive. And governments are increasingly ill disposed toward financial types, as they were in the 1930s.

The smart move for all those MBA graduates would have been to earn agriculture and mining degrees. More people today study public relations than study agriculture; more study phys ed or sports management than study mining engineering. But farming, in the future, is going to be a far more rewarding sector of the economy than finance. Soon, stockbrokers will be driving taxis—or the smart ones will be driving tractors in order to work for the farmers—while the farmers will be driving Lamborghinis.

(Lamborghini, which still manufactures the vehicles, started out as a tractor company.) Ferruccio Lamborghini founded the original company, Lamborghini Trattori, in 1948, building his first tractors from surplus automobile engines and leftover military hardware, and soon became one of the larger manufacturers of agricultural equipment in Italy. He started Automobili Lamborghini in 1963. I had always heard that it was because he had approached Enzo Ferrari to buy one of his cars, but Signor Ferrari sneered that he did not want tractor drivers to be seen in his cars. Necessity being the mother of invention, Ferruccio made his own cars.)

We are in a long secular bull market in commodities worldwide. In the last bull market in commodities and agriculture in the 1970s, with prices of food rising dramatically, large inventories developed. By the 1980s, inventories of food worldwide were something like 35 percent of consumption, which is maybe the highest in recorded history. Prices eventually plummeted as a result. The price of sugar, for example, fell from 66 cents a pound in 1974 to two cents a pound in 1987. Farmers everywhere were suffering, so much so that in the United States, musicians like Willie Nelson were organizing Farm Aid concerts. As a sector of the economy, farming was a disaster, and every future farmer of America grabbed one of those MBAs and went to Wall Street instead. That is where the money was. That is where the action was.

But times have changed. The average age of farmers in the United States now is fifty-nine years old. In ten years those farmers will be sixty-nine, if they are still alive. In Japan, the average age today is even higher: sixty-seven. Farms there have dried up. If you drive around the country, you will see huge empty fields. Japanese farmers, those who are still alive, have aged, and their kids are in Tokyo or Osaka working as stockbrokers. The situation has grown so desperate in Japan, one of the more chauvinistic countries in the world, that the government has allowed

Chinese farmers to enter the country to farm the fields on an experimental basis. Things have been even worse in India. Because farming has been such a terrible place to make a living, hundreds of thousands of Indian farmers have committed suicide over the past decade and a half. On average, one farmer commits suicide every thirty minutes in India, according to a report cited by *Forbes* magazine in May 2011.

Until prices reach a point where growing food is profitable, the world's farmers, who are currently aging and dying, are not going to be replaced. Prices must rise, and they will. In recent years, the world has been consuming more food than it has produced. Those inventories that were so high in the 1980s are now historically low, somewhere near 14 percent of consumption. The world is facing dramatic shortages. Food prices are on the way up. Complain all you want. If they do not rise much higher, we are going to experience something we have never experienced before—no food at any price.

The current bull market in commodities began in 1999. We are fourteen years into it, at the time of this writing. Like all bull markets, it will end in a bubble. When, at cocktail parties, people are telling you how much money they made in soybeans, it will be time to get out. But the bull market still has several years to go. Commodities, raw materials, and natural resources will do well, obviously, if the world economy improves—growth will spur a need for them—and they will do well if the economy does *not* improve, because the government, though it should not, will print more money, as it has shown, and printing money has always led to stronger prices for real goods, such as silver, rice, energy, and other real assets, as investors seek to protect themselves from debased currency.

But that is another story, one I will get to later.

To those students attending my lecture at Balliol in 2010 who were still determined to work in finance, I explained how the study of philosophy and history were indispensable to me as an investor. "You must know yourself better," I told them, "if you want to accomplish anything in life—you must learn to think at a deeper, more profound level if you want to understand the truth." The study of philosophy helped me develop these skills. Studying philosophy trained me to think for myself, to think outside the established framework. It taught me to examine things independently, to examine every concept and every "fact." It taught me to think around corners, to see what is missing. So many people today are caught up in conventional thinking because it is easier and safer to echo perceived wisdom, to echo the opinion of the majority, with one's intellectual processes circumscribed by such concepts as the state, culture, or religion. To think differently from others is difficult. Philosophy teaches you to think, and in doing so it teaches you to doubt.

If history teaches us nothing else, it teaches us this: what appears undisputed today will look very different tomorrow. The most stable and predictable societies have undergone major upheavals. The Austro-Hungarian Empire, the glittering jewel of central Europe, was a vast, international center of wealth in 1914. The Vienna stock exchange at the time had something like four thousand members. Within four years the Austro-Hungarian Empire disappeared. Pick any year you want, and then move forward ten or fifteen years. Take 1925, when again widespread peace, prosperity, and stability prevailed. How did things look in 1935? In 1940? Pick the first year of any decade in the past fifty years, 1960, 1970, all the way through to the millennium. The conventional wisdom that existed at the start of each decade was shattered over the following ten or fifteen years.

WHILE A STUDENT at Oxford I did not do as much traveling as I would have liked, for lack of money, but it was there that my urge to travel was first rewarded. The academic year in England is punctuated by two six-week holidays, one at Christmas and one at Easter. Because, for the same lack of funds, I could not fly home my first Christmas, I hitched a ride with two other Americans who had a car and were driving to Morocco. We split up in Madrid. While they proceeded south, I hitchhiked to Lisbon, then down to Gibraltar, where I was to rendezvous with them on their way back to Oxford. When their ferry landed at Gibraltar, they had three young American women with them in the car.

One of the three was a nice, proper Jewish girl from Philadelphia named Lois. She had just graduated from the University of Pennsylvania. She had a relative, a doctor, who was attached to the US Embassy in Copenhagen, and she was staying there with him and his family while touring Europe. She was headed to Denmark. About three hundred kilometers into the trip back north, the car broke down, and though it took some effort, I persuaded Lois to hitchhike with me as far as Paris, where she would pick up a train to Copenhagen and from where I would continue on to Oxford. We spent three or four nights together on the road—she slept in two pairs of ski pants—and in Paris, just before we split up, we grabbed a meal together on the way to the train station.

"You can't leave yet," I told her. "You haven't eaten everything on your plate."

"I'm twenty-two years old," she said. "I don't have to eat everything on my plate."

"When you were a little girl," I said, "didn't your parents tell you to think about all the poor starving children in China?"

"When I was a little girl," she said, "my parents told me to think about all the poor starving children in Alabama."

By the time of my second Christmas in Oxford, Lois had rented an apartment there. In the summer, we hitchhiked to Yugoslavia together, and after that we joined a three-week student tour for which I had signed up, taking us to five other Communist countries. We traveled to East Germany, Poland, Czechoslovakia, Ukraine, and Russia. These trips afforded me my first look at life behind the Iron Curtain and my first real-world look at how the black market works.

The Russian ruble was not a convertible currency. You could not buy and sell it in the market. It was not legal to import rubles into, or take them out of, the Soviet Union. But the American Express office in London had rubles, and you could buy them there at a huge discount—just as you could on the black market inside Russia—receiving maybe five times the official rate. We bought a bunch of rubles in London, Lois stuffed them into her brassiere, and we smuggled them into Russia. The goods and services available in the country, cheap by Western standards, as limited as they happened to be, were that much cheaper for us. Years later, when driving around the world, whenever I crossed outlying borders, one of the first things I would do was find the black market.

By our third Christmas together, Lois and I were married—although her parents were most unhappy that I was not Jewish—and I had my sights set on Wall Street.

3

ON MY OWN

In 1966, nobody in Marengo County was going to get out of the draft. The draft board was just one lady, and her two sons, who had been called up, had both been killed in combat, serving in earlier wars than the one being waged in Vietnam at the time. I was very much against the war, and one might have expected the same of her, but her sacrifice had hardened rather than softened her support for the conflict. Before heading to Wall Street, I would fulfill a two-year military obligation.

Signing up for Officers Candidate School, I was allowed to choose my branch, so I chose the army Quartermaster Corps, and after boot camp I was sent to school at Fort Lee, Virginia. Lois at the time was getting her PhD at Columbia, and as often as possible she came down from New York to be with me. Graduating at the top of my OCS class, I was able to select my posting, and the one quartermaster posting available in New York, which was where I wanted to be assigned, was at Fort Hamilton in Brooklyn. I got the posting; I was stationed there, where, with another young lieutenant, I managed the Officers Club.

In conversation with my commanding officer it came out that, when my tour was up, I was going to work on Wall Street. This was 1968 and stocks were going through the roof; people everywhere were crowing about how much money they were making, so the commanding officer asked me to help him out with his investments, and I agreed. I thought I knew what I was doing. Fortunately, I did not lose his money. I actually made him a little bit. By the time I left the army in August 1968, I had returned his investment in cash along with the profits. I do not know what he did with it after that. Later in '68 the bull market peaked. Wall Street collapsed, and a long bear market followed. But I had left him in good shape.

I LANDED ON WALL STREET at the start of a decade that would prove to be one of the dreariest in the history of the market. The collapse of the Dow in 1970 was the worst since the 1930s. I worked a couple of years as an analyst at three different firms before being hired that year by Arnhold and S. Bleichroeder, an old German Jewish investment firm of the highest caliber. (Gerson von Bleichroeder had been the banker to Bismarck.) In 1937, with the rise of the Nazis, the company had moved its operations to New York, and it was there, in its small, family-run office, that I really spread my wings.

The beauty, the excitement of Wall Street, is that things are always changing. You have to stay ahead of events. The action is never ending. It is like a four-dimensional puzzle, linked to volume and time. Every day you come in to work and find that they have moved the pieces on you—somebody dies, there is a strike or a war, weather conditions have shifted. Things change, no matter what. Investing lacks the rhythm of other endeavors, and therefore never stops testing you: if you design a car, there is a predictable period of time in which you produce the car and sell it, and the market will either accept it or reject it, but at least the project has a life span. With investing, nothing stops moving, and that makes it a continual, ongoing challenge . . . a game, a battle . . . call it what you will.

I loved every minute of it. I was in my element. And I worked all the time, seven days a week sometimes. I remember occasionally wishing that the stock market did not close on weekends—I loved it that much. I can remember visiting ten companies in ten cities in a single week. There was no such thing as too much time doing this. Lois, understandably, hated how much I worked. While I was putting in fifteen-hour days at the office, she was caught up in the student demonstrations on the Columbia campus, where Wall Street was in bad repute. She did not understand this crazy, driven, ambitious boy who wanted to make his fortune there. By the time I arrived at Bleichroeder, she and I were divorced. (Not until leaving campus did Lois and many of her fellow students learn about real life. Neither Lois's parents nor her forty-year-old brother would guarantee a car loan for her upon graduation, so she asked me. I also declined.)

Four and a half years later I married again, and again,

because of my single-minded focus on work, the marriage was brief. I am not particularly proud of it but I was never what one might call "good relationship material." I was fifty-seven when I married Paige, and not until then did I have staying power with women. I was always in and out of relationships, including my first two marriages. Paige is clearly special, since she could and can put up with me. I am one of five brothers—we have no sisters—and we all but one have divorces in our lives. In passing conversations with my brothers, I find that none of us ever received parental advice about how to deal with the opposite sex. And I do not think that either of my parents would have known what to tell us if we had asked. Both were just out of their teens when they married, and neither had much experience dating. Knowing the shortcomings of my own education—self-awareness came late in life—I hope to do better by my daughters. All parents need to teach their children the basics of relationships, and as the girls develop I hope to offer them insights and advice. I will try to give them the benefit of my experience, having myself learned things the hard way.

Hard work on Wall Street is a given. But those who succeed are few. A lot of people make a lot of money during the bull market years, but doing it under normal conditions is tougher, and doing it in a bear market harder still. Most people get bounced out of the industry. Persistence and perseverance are absolutely essential to survival, but just as important is judgment.

To succeed on Wall Street, you have to be extremely curious. Who knows, when you pick up a rock, what might crawl out and where it will lead? Furthermore, you have to be skeptical. Most of the things you are told, after turning over that rock, are going to be inaccurate, reflecting a lack of knowledge or a distortion of information, whether on the part of government, a company, or an individual. You cannot take anybody's word for anything. You have to research everything yourself, prove everything yourself. You have to tap every source. A hundred people can walk into a room and hear the same information at the same time, but only 3 or 4 percent of them are going to come out of there and make the right judgment.

When I started on Wall Street, very few people invested in stocks. As late as the 1960s, individual and institutional investors, such as pension plans and endowments, invested chiefly in bonds. (Currencies and commodities? Few people on Wall Street could even spell those words.) The Ford Foundation commissioned a study at the end of the 1960s that concluded that "common stocks" were adequate investments, that the combination of dividends and capital gains made them as attractive as bonds. A new world emerged as investors came into the market acting on these findings, thanks to the foundation's credibility. It is inconceivable to today's MBAs that common stocks were an uncommon investment only a few decades ago. But not until the bull market started in the 1980s did things change in a big way. Today nearly all institutions have most of their investments in stocks. Back when I started in 1964, a big day at the New York Stock Exchange was three million shares. Three million shares is one trade today. They might do three million shares before breakfast, and that is before the exchange opens. The volume now is something like five billion shares a week, plus another five billion or so on NASDAQ.

Back then, all anybody knew, if they knew stocks at all, were those stocks listed on the New York Stock Exchange. Few Americans were investing abroad. The Second World War had devastated much of the rest of the world, and people in the United States, the one rich and powerful country, had yet to start looking for opportunities there. There were various reasons for this limited view, but nothing discouraged investment more than the exchange controls that existed at the time, including those in the United States.

In 1962, with Germany's economy growing, the Japanese becoming more self-sufficient, and other countries' economies improving, a lot of dollars were leaving the Unites States. We were buying more and more goods from abroad, and a balance of trade problem was developing. So in 1963, Congress, in its (lack of) wisdom, imposed something called the interest equalization tax, a 15 percent tax on any investment outside the United States made by US residents. If you bought shares of Volkswagen for $100, you paid $100 for the shares and $15 to the US government. The tax was designed to discourage investment abroad. And it did that. There were not many people investing overseas, despite the opportunities. The rest of the world was booming—at America's expense.

I had been interested in international investing since my Oxford days. It was then that I had first begun seeing what was going on in the rest of the world. I remember getting out of the army in 1968, talking about investing in things like the Danish krone, and the people around me not having a clue as to what I was going on about. All these smart, experienced older guys were just dumbfounded. It seemed as if they did not know where Denmark was, much less that it presented an opportunity. There were only two firms on Wall Street, small companies, that specialized in foreign investing, and Arnhold and S. Bleichroeder was one of them. (The other was Carl Marks & Co.)

I was hired at Bleichroeder to work with a vice president of the firm, George Soros. He had been looking for a bright young fellow, while I was looking to change jobs. Somebody introduced us, and we hit it off right away. He had the same international outlook that I did. About twelve years older than I, Soros had grown up in Hungary, lived in the United Kingdom until his mid-twenties, and had a background in international investing, so we made a good team. We were managing a fund at Bleichroeder, the Double Eagle hedge fund, taking advantage of huge opportunities at home and abroad, when due to a technical change in the industry, a new regulatory restriction, we were forced to split from the firm and go out on our own. Arnhold and S. Bleichroeder would remain our primary broker.

We got a little office and created the Quantum Fund, a sophisticated, offshore hedge fund for foreign investors—who were not subject to the interest equalization tax—incorporated in the Netherlands Antilles. We bought and sold short stocks, commodities, currencies, and bonds located anywhere in the world. We invested where others did not, exploiting untapped markets around the globe. I worked ceaselessly, making myself master as much as possible of the worldwide flow of capital, goods, raw materials, and information.

By 1974, there were only a handful of hedge funds left in the world. There had not been many to start with, and most had gone out of business because Wall Street was such a terrible place to make money. Even the few that existed invested mainly in the United States. We were the only international hedge fund. In theory, the hedge fund guys are the smart guys, but none of them were investing abroad at the time. Back then not many could find Belgium on a map, much less exploit it.

The original hedge fund was structured in 1949 by Alfred Winslow Jones. The fund was around when we started our fund—A.W. Jones is still around today—and had been very successful in the 1950s and 1960s. We used the same compensation structure that Jones had come up with and that other people were using at the time.

The chief difference between a hedge fund and a mutual fund, of course, is stated in the name: the ability to hedge. Hedge funds can sell short. Mutual funds in the United States just buy shares. That is all they do. They are long only. They are restricted by SEC compensation rules to charging low fees, and they are not allowed to borrow money—that is, to buy on margin. Hedge funds can buy on margin and they can charge whatever they want. We charged 1 percent of the assets as an annual management fee—a mutual fund might have charged 0.5 percent—and, as an incentive fee, 20 percent of any profits that accrued, which was standard in those days.

Hedge funds, theoretically, would always make money, in

good years and bad, because they could sell short. And that is where the incentive fee came in. If you did well, you could make a lot of money. If there were no profits, investors paid nothing. But it was likely that there were going to be significant profits, and investors were happy to pay the 20 percent, because it meant that they were making money, too.

After the war, A.W. Jones went to investors and said, "I am a smart guy; I am going to set up this fund where I will hedge my bets, our bets, and since I am a good investor, I expect you to pay me a lot to do well. If you want to invest with me, you have to pay." Mutual funds were not (and are not) allowed to charge incentive fees. But according to a provision in the law, if you had fewer than ninety-nine investors, you were not considered to be raising money from the public—unlike Fidelity, for instance, which was raising money from millions of investors—and private parties could make any kind of compensation arrangement they wanted. Hedge funds, therefore, were structured to be small.

Soros was a very good trader, had a very good sense of market timing and trading, at which I was not good and cared little about. I did most of the research. What interested me was turning over the rocks and pursuing leads, discovering what was going on in the world and predicting where things were headed. This was the passion of mine that had been rewarded back in 1964 when I had stumbled onto Wall Street, finding work I would have done for nothing if simultaneously I could have found a way to support myself.

I cut my salary dramatically to go off on this venture. I took a 75 percent pay cut. But the money was irrelevant to me. The advice I give everyone, the advice I will give my children, is this: before asking how much you are going to get paid for a job, first decide whether it is the right job, whether it is the right place for you, because if it is the right place and you do the job right, the money will come. The money will find you, I assure you. The money should be the least of your questions.

There we were in a little office off Columbus Circle at the corner of Central Park, just the three of us, including the secretary, and things went right. We did everything: we invested all over the world—stocks, bonds, currencies, commodities—we sold short, we borrowed money, we did everything a person could do in the financial markets. We did things anybody else could have done, things other people were not doing, because they were discouraged by exchange controls and by their limited view of history. America, geographically, had been, and to some extent still is, isolated. We have these two oceans on either side of us. We were the only country that had any kind of money after the war. We did not have much intercourse with the rest of the world; we did not need to. We were triumphant. Why would American investors even think of Germany, France, Italy, or Japan, which had come out of the war devastated?

Insatiably curious about the world, I was looking for whatever I could find. We agreed that the opportunities were out there, and if you find them, you invest. We were not constrained by history or geography, by tradition or similar absurdities. We invested wherever we saw opportunities, which meant we invested all over the world. We used a lot of leverage—we borrowed a lot of money to make the investments—which entailed substantial risk, but fortunately we did it right. Certainly we were right more often than we were wrong.

One of our early traumas came in 1971, when President Nixon closed the gold window by refusing to let other governments swap their US dollars for our gold. He simultaneously instituted wage and price controls and imposed a 10 percent surcharge on imported goods. We were long Japanese stocks. Japan had been booming. It was a wonderfully overlooked market. It was cheap, it was growing, and its currency was sound. We had invested in Japan and we were short in the United States. Our shorts were mainly US stocks. Nixon made the announcement on Sunday night. That week the Japanese stock market, where we were long, went down 20 percent and the American market, where we were short, went through the roof. We suffered badly that week. But we also had some North Sea oil. It offset our losses. Production was coming onstream, and we were investing in European oil companies. They were thriving, poised to make a fortune from the North Sea.

WHILE IT IS the most widely traded commodity, and probably the most important commodity—one of the more important assets of any kind—oil did not trade on a commodity exchange until the 1980s. In the 1970s, and for decades before that, before the New York Mercantile Exchange provided an open market in crude, oil traded over the telephone, with brokers or with people in the energy business. Other commodities for which there are huge markets, like paper, steel, and uranium, have never generated sufficient interest among the people within those industries to be traded on an exchange. Coal has been around for hundreds of years, but the people who buy and sell it are still content to conduct their transactions without benefit of an organized market.

As early as 1971, two years before energy prices started rising dramatically, Quantum was investing in oil and natural gas. My research showed that serious shortages were developing. I received a prospectus that year from a company issuing thirty-year bonds for the development of a natural gas pipeline, in which it was pointed out, in the very same prospectus, that the company's natural gas reserves at the time amounted to eight years' worth of supply—after which, one had to assume, there would be nothing to go through the pipeline unless something changed. The industry had been running gas reserves down for years, largely because very little money could be made from drilling for natural gas.

In 1956, the United States Supreme Court had ruled it legal for the federal government to set the price of natural gas flowing through interstate pipelines, and the price had been set (and in 1971 remained) very low. In 1956, at fourteen years old, I had known little about the Supreme Court, but I was not unacquainted with the oil fields of the American Southwest. I can still remember driving with my parents from Alabama to Oklahoma, where my mother's family lived, and passing the drilling fields of Louisiana and Texas. And I saw fires burning everywhere. Flames shot up from the drilling rigs as the oil men burned off the gas while pumping the oil. The price of natural gas made it hardly worth saving. Oil, as cheap as it was at the time, was much more lucrative.

Of course, I did not understand any of that at the time, but the memory of the burning fields was vivid in 1971, when, after receiving the pipeline prospectus, I read the annual report of a company called Helmerich & Payne, a large drilling contractor. The company, which had been in business for decades, reported that the number of drilling rigs in the United States had declined every year for the previous fifteen. Steadily, since 1956, both gas and oil companies, it appeared, had been tapping reserves. It was becoming clear to me that we faced a serious energy problem in the United States and, by extrapolation, the world.

I went to see the chairman of Helmerich & Payne. He took me aside—I was twenty-nine years old—and he said, "Listen, this is a terrible business. I just want to alert you. I am here, this is my family company, and obviously I am not going to leave, but you really should not be investing in this business." In the annual report that I had read, he had explained the downturn in business as something beyond the company's control—there had been a long decline in the number of drilling rigs, the report stated, because drilling for gas or oil had not been profitable. And that just excited me more. Everywhere I went I could see that supplies were drying up.

We went out and invested in all of it.

I told a friend of mine who worked at a fund what we were doing based on what I had learned—a fellow who had attended Harvard Business School and who wore it on his sleeve that he had attended Harvard Business School—and he dismissed my analysis. A couple of years later, after the 1973 Arab-Israeli War and the subsequent oil embargo initiated by the Arab members of OPEC, he and I bumped into each other.

"Boy, you guys really were lucky, weren't you," he said.

"What are you talking about?" I said. "I told you this was happening. I told you why it would happen. It did happen. And now you say it's luck."

"If it had not been for the war," he insisted, "prices would not have gone up."

And then I tried to educate him all over again.

I pointed out that the embargo had been lifted after five months, and yet the price continued to climb. OPEC had been formed in 1960, I reminded him, and every year the ministers met and every year they raised the price of oil, only to see the market laugh at them and to watch the price go down. But here, in 1973, when they raised the price, it stuck. Why? Because shortages were developing. Nobody was drilling for oil. Reserve supplies were running out. People invested, the markets reacted, and things went up.

The fundamentals were right. You can invest in something all day long, but unless the fundamentals are right, it is not going to take you anywhere. Get the fundamentals right and the good news keeps coming. Lucky? If you want to be lucky, do your homework.

As Louis Pasteur pointed out, "Luck favors only the mind that is prepared."

I HAD NOTICED in the opening days of the Arab-Israeli War that the Egyptian Air Force was succeeding in shooting Israeli jets out of the sky, which made no sense to me—Israel's Air Force was far superior—and I tried to figure out why. I learned that it was because the Egyptians were deploying advanced electronic-warfare equipment they had received from the Soviets. I jumped on a plane and started visiting defense contractors around the country. Lockheed, which at the time was in bankruptcy (having overextended as it failed to compete successfully with Boeing), was famous for its Advanced Development Projects division, better known as the Skunk Works, located in California, where its engineers came up with sophisticated weaponry for the Pentagon. I investigated Lockheed and other companies, like Northrop. I flew to Washington and learned that even the doves in Congress—Democratic senator William Proxmire from Wisconsin being one of those to whom I talked—were in favor of Pentagon spending on advanced electronic warfare. With government defense spending under pressure following the Vietnam War, defense stocks at the time were depressed—selling for a dollar, two dollars, some of them—and adding what my research showed to the fact that they were so cheap, we started buying a lot of those stocks.

Around this time, a group of young hotshot investors in New York who got together once a month to have dinner, recommend investments, and share their views on the world invited me to attend one of their gatherings. I had heard of some of these guys and was very excited to be there among them. I started explaining why we owned Lockheed, which was selling for something in the vicinity of two dollars, and I remember a guy at the far end of the table announcing in a loud stage whisper how absurd he thought I was, expressing how much disdain he had for such an investment strategy. He had his own hedge fund, one of the few that existed at the time—theoretically making him the better hotshot—and for that reason, and because it was my first dinner with all these guys, I was very much embarrassed. His name was Bruce Waterfall. He was about my age. His company was Morgens Waterfall. (He died in 2008.) Lockheed went up a hundred times over the next few years. I would remember Waterfall's reaction, because it was the reception I would continue to get whenever I talked out loud about the things I was investing in.

At Quantum, running against the conventional wisdom, Soros and I shorted those large-cap, buy-and-hold growth stocks that were considered extremely stable, known as the Nifty Fifty—some were selling at one hundred times earnings, two hundred times earnings, all the banks, all the mutual funds were buying them . . . We shorted the pound sterling . . . In 1980, gold was on a tear—we shorted it. They were glorious and exciting years; we had gains every year. And those were the days of the bear market, when everybody thought Wall Street was a horrible place to be. In 1980, after a decade in which the S & P 500 rose 47 percent—approximating the gains my mother realized in her passbook savings account at the local bank—the Quantum portfolio was up 4,200 percent.

4

BEATING THE BEAR MARKET

In the mid-1970s, I attended a party on Central Park West thrown by investment manager Jeff Tarr and his wife, Patsy. When asked by Mrs. Tarr what I did for a living, I told her I worked on Wall Street. Her immediate response was one of commiseration.

"Oh," she said, "you must be suffering."

The markets were terrible, had been bad for years, and, alas, would continue to be bad—in 1964, the Dow had ended the year at 800, and in 1982 it would still be 800, following eighteen years of record inflation.

"No," I assured her, "things are great. I'm short."

As she looked me up and down, her expression made clear what she was thinking:

I can see you're short, you fool, but what does that have to do with anything?

Although there certainly had been a time when, at five feet five and a half inches, I was self-conscious about my height, it had long since passed by then. Any insecurity I had disappeared around the time I joined the army. The shortest member of my OCS class—we always lined up by height—I was nonetheless the leader by virtue of my performance as first in the class. Later, independence and success, both financial and romantic, only served to make my height that much more irrelevant. I remember reminding my girlfriend Tabitha, at five feet ten inches insecure about her own height, to "stand up straight," and not worry about towering over me. I explained she did not have to worry about height anymore.

Hedge funds at the time were few, and selling short, which, among other things, is how hedge funds hedge their bets, was relatively unknown. Mrs. Tarr was not alone, back then, in being unfamiliar with the practice. Among the many people to whom the concept was a mystery was President Richard Nixon. When selling short was explained to him, Nixon denounced it as un-American. And he was not the first political leader in history who considered it unpatriotic. Napoleon Bonaparte imprisoned short sellers for treason.

Most people buy a stock at, say, 10 and sell it at, say, 25. They buy and sell to make a profit. Selling short reverses the process by which the profit is made. You sell the stock at 25 and then buy it at 10. How do you sell it if you do not first have it? You borrow the stock from somebody. I go to J.P. Morgan and borrow 100 shares of stock and sell the stock at 25, which is its current market price. I sell it because I think it will be going down in value. So when it goes to 10, I buy 100 shares and give them to J.P. Morgan. The bank has its 100 shares back, I have my profit, and the world goes on.

Short selling is in fact indispensable to the market. It adds liquidity as well as stability. The market needs both buyers and sellers. Without sellers, prices can skyrocket; without buyers, prices collapse. Suppose everybody, caught up in the dot-com mania, wants to buy a stock like Cisco. The stock goes from 20 to 80. The short sellers start coming in. The stock might then go to 90. Without short sellers, it would go to 110. Without short sellers, there would be no sellers at all—there would be no liquidity, things would go nuts. Short sellers temper the mania.

Let us say the short sellers are wrong. They have to cover their shorts, and they are summarily forced out of the market. And the stock goes to where it would have gone anyway. But suppose the short sellers are right—and, by the way, short sellers have a better record than most on Wall Street—and the stock starts heading toward a collapse. Everyone is in a panic, begging to get out. Everyone is screaming to sell. But with the stock crashing, there are no buyers. Well, there is one group of buyers, actually: the short sellers. They have to buy back the stock. They have to replace the stock they borrowed. They have to cover their shorts. So in the collapse, the stock does not drop as much as it might have. A stock that might have gone down to 3 goes down only to, say, 8.

So short sellers are good for the market. They have saved you from buying the failed stock at 110—if you bought at the top, you bought at 90, instead—and when you dump, thanks to the short seller, you will be able to get out at 8 rather than 3. Short selling has prevailed for some four hundred years because, after being tested repeatedly in the marketplace, it has shown itself to be valuable.

To politicians, who have scapegoated it over the centuries, short selling has proved to be very useful. When things go south, they can fall back on blaming the evil speculators. When the stock market is dropping from 1,000 to 500 and people are losing their jobs, going bankrupt everywhere you look, no politician is going to say, "My God, I have messed up, I am going to resign." No, it is the fault of those evil short sellers on Wall Street.

During an interview I gave on CNBC in 2008, it was known that I had shorted mortgage lender Fannie Mae. I had been talking about it for a year or two: that Fannie Mae was a sham and on the verge of collapse. I had written in my book *Hot Commodities*, published four years earlier, that both Fannie Mae and Freddie Mac were scandals-in-waiting. So here it was, 2008, and Fannie Mae stock was going from 60 to bankrupt. It was down to 20 by then, and the correspondent interviewing me—the reporter for a business channel, mind you—opined that the collapse was my fault.

"Listen," I told the reporter, as politely as I could, "if you really think that Fannie Mae is going into the tank because of short sellers, you really should get another job."

The lack of understanding was something I had come to expect of the man on the street—not everyone, as I said, is familiar with short selling—but such ignorance on the part of a television business reporter came as a surprise, even to me. Short sellers are not the cause; they are simply the messengers, and as such they have exposed many of the great frauds. The criminal enterprise that was Enron is one of the more famous scandals they are responsible for having identified.

SHORT SELLING IS not for the casual player on Wall Street. It demands a little bit more knowledge; it calls for more serious homework. Only the well informed need apply. A stock you might buy at 10 can go down only to zero. You can lose only 100 percent. But sell a stock short at 10, and your losses are theoretically unlimited—it can go to 20, to 30, to 40, to 50; it could go to 1,000. Selling short can hurt you very badly and very quickly if you are wrong.

I went broke doing it early in my career.

In 1970, I had come to the conclusion that the stock market was going to collapse. I took all my money and bought puts— options that gave me the right to sell at a certain price for a certain amount of time, limiting my losses in a way that short selling did not. One pays a premium to do this, but one also gets greater leverage, if things do go down. Five months later the stock market collapsed. Firms that had been around for decades were going out of business; it was the worst collapse since 1937. On the day the market hit bottom, I sold my puts. I took my profits, if you will. I tripled my money.

Here I was, a snotty-nosed kid, thinking I knew what I was doing. I said, well, what I am going to do now is wait, because the market is going to rally. I do not know if I was showing wisdom beyond my years, but sure enough the market rallied, and after waiting two months I took all the money I had made on my puts and I sold short. I decided that I was not going to pay the premium anymore, that I was just going to sell short, and I shorted six different companies, anticipating another drop. And two months later, I was wiped out.

As the companies' stock prices had continued to rise, I had been forced to keep covering my shorts because I did not have sufficient holdings in my brokerage account to hang on until prices started to fall. I did not have the staying power that short selling requires. I did not have the resources to stay with it; to say, OK, they are wrong and I am right. I had to reverse my position, and I lost everything I had. I had been forced to cover before I owed money. One thing about Wall Street, if you are trading on margin: the brokers will reverse your position before you go into debt; they always make sure they are covered.

Within the next two or three years, every one of those six companies I had shorted went bankrupt, and I was a genius. Which put me in mind of the saying "If you're so smart, then why aren't you rich?"

This was a perfect example of being smart and not being rich. I had been so smart I went broke. I did not know what the markets were capable of.

On Wall Street there is no truer adage, I learned, than the one attributed erroneously to John Maynard Keynes: "Markets can remain irrational longer than you can remain solvent."

Keynes, by the way, was both smart and rich; he was one of the great stock market speculators of all time. He knew what he was doing. With the King's College, Cambridge, endowment and with his own money, he speculated almost full-time, and he was very successful. When he died in 1946, he was worth more than half a million pounds, the equivalent of over $16 million today.

I had been smart and had lost everything for being so smart.

The experience was a valuable one. It taught me how little I knew about markets. And it taught me a lot about myself. Later, during a brief tenure at Columbia University, I would share the lesson with students. Do not worry about failure, I would tell them. Do not worry about making mistakes in life. It is good to lose money, to go broke at least once, and preferably twice. But if you are going to do it, do it early in your career. It is better to go bust when you are talking about $20,000 than when you are talking about $20 million. Do it early, and it is not the end of the world.

Losing everything can be a beneficial experience, because it teaches you how much you do not know. And if you can come back from a failure or two, chances are you are going to be more successful in the long run. There are countless stories of very successful people who failed once, twice, three times, and then came back. Mike Bloomberg got fired from Salomon Brothers, and it was the best thing that ever happened to him. He started his own company, delivering business information, and now he is one of the richest guys in the world. There is nothing wrong with failing if you learn from your mistakes.

One of the more obvious mistakes I had made in shorting those six companies was assuming that everybody knew what I knew. I had come in much too early. Since then I have learned to wait, or try to, at any rate. But manias can rise to levels that are impossible to conceive, and as I discovered, I am not very good at figuring out that moment when suddenly everybody else realizes that what is happening is insane.

IF YOU WERE to walk into a cocktail party in Manhattan today, you would be hard-pressed to find anyone who does not know what a hedge fund is or what selling short entails. The staggering growth of hedge funds and mutual funds in the financial industry, a product of the bull market of the 1980s and 1990s, has every American with a retirement account following the markets. In 2010, according to the Investment Company Institute, some seventy thousand mutual funds existed worldwide, more than seventy-five hundred of them in the United States. In a 2011 Gallup poll, 54 percent of Americans said they had money invested in the stock market. In 2007, before the financial crisis, that number was 65 percent.

More than half the people in the United States have money invested in the market, and it is nothing short of astonishing how little so many of them know, how many of them there are who have absolutely no clue what they are doing. No wonder they lose money—they know nothing about investing, and yet they go off and do it, and they do it expecting to make fortunes. My advice to them is this: put your money in the bank and earn 1 or 2 percent interest. It is better than *losing* 1 or 2 percent interest. If you do not believe me, try it for a few years, and I promise you will see the difference.

People are constantly asking me what to invest in, and I always answer the same way. I say: Do not listen to me—do not listen to anybody. The way you become a successful investor is by investing only in what you yourself have a wealth of knowledge about. Everybody knows a lot about something. Cars, fashion, whatever it is—you know a lot about something. If you do not know what it is you know a lot about, just step back and take a look at your daily life. When you walk into a doctor's waiting room, what magazines do you pick up? If you turn on a television, what kinds of programs do you watch? Soon you will probably figure out what your real interests are, what you are really knowledgeable about.

Now you are ready to become a successful investor. If you are keen on cars, read everything you can about the automobile industry. You will know when something is about to happen that constitutes a major, positive change. Then start following up. Read more about whatever you find. Maybe a new fuel-injection system is being developed, one that is superior to and cheaper than that which is currently in use, and you know that when it goes into production, it will take up a large share of the market. Or it could be something like a new highway. Maybe people can drive someplace where they could never drive before. Maybe new hotels or shopping centers are certain to open up there. The fundamental strategy is this: stay with what you know and expand on it. If somebody calls you up and says, oh, my gosh, there is this great new computer process . . . ignore it. You do not know anything about computers. Cars are what you know. Concentrate on what you know and any changes you see—you will see a major change coming long before I ever will, long before anybody on Wall Street will, because cars are your passion; they are what you are sitting around reading about all the time.

Learn to think in the appropriate terms: this is something new; this is something different; this is a shift in direction. Anything new or different leads to consequences down the road. You have to learn to think around corners. You will know before anybody on Wall Street when something good is happening. You will know it is time to buy. You will also know when to sell, because you will see before anybody else that the great change you noticed a few years ago is starting to reverse itself—someone is building a cheaper product, the Chinese are building a better product, the competition has intensified. You will know it is time to sell long before the people on Wall Street.

Let us say you have done that. You have pursued your interest, your passion. You have capitalized on your knowledge. You have stayed with what you know, expanded on it, and you have enjoyed tremendous success. After ten years you have made ten times your money. And then you decide to sell. Now, that is a very dangerous time. It is dangerous because that is when you think you are really smart, when you think you are really hot. It is the time when you think you know that this investing thing is an easy game. It is the time you should open the curtains, look out the window, go to the beach, do anything but think about investing. Because now is when you are most vulnerable. You think: *I have to find something else. I have to do it again. This is wonderful. This is so easy.* Just as I thought after tripling my money with my puts.

It is the great mistake people make. Now and then a time comes when doing nothing is the wisest course. Most successful investors, in fact, do nothing most of the time. Do not confuse movement with action. Know when to sit and wait. (I am sitting and waiting right now.) You bought that stock ten years ago, and you did nothing for the next ten years—you did nothing but watch what was going on, nothing but watch for changes. That is how you make money. Now, after you sell the stock, it is just as important to do nothing. Just wait patiently. Wait until you see money lying over there in the corner.

If you were walking around the house and you saw money lying over in the corner, and all you had to do was go over and pick it up . . . ? That is the kind of investment you should make. You should wait until you find something you are so thoroughly sure of, based on your wealth of knowledge, and something that is so cheap, that buying it is as foolproof as going over to the corner and picking up the money. That is what successful investors do. They do not do a lot of jumping around. Warren Buffett rarely changes his holdings. I do not change my positions a lot since I invest in secular trends, which by definition last many years.

If I were to tell you that you could make only twenty-five investments in your lifetime, chances are you would be extremely careful about investing. Most people jump from here to there—they have to do this, they have to do that, they heard a hot tip over here, their brother-in-law told them that over there. . . . If you are a short-term day trader, then sure, go ahead, but successful short-term day traders are few and far between. If, on the other hand, you are an investor, you should be as careful as you would be if you had only twenty-five investments to make over the course of your life. That is the way investors make money.

To invest in stocks, bonds, or commodities, to invest in just

about anything, you have to have a brokerage account, an investment account, and that means you have to find a broker. And all
you need to know about the broker is whether he (or she) is solvent.
You do not want to ask him for advice. Because he does not know
nearly so much as you know about what it is you want to buy. He
may never even have heard of it. Remember, you are the first person to realize that this is going to be a good thing. You tell him you
want to buy a hundred shares, a thousand shares, whatever it is,
of XYZ Inc. And then you sit and wait. You constantly have to confirm your research, the original insight you had, because the stock
is going to be jumping around in price all the time, and the world
is always going to be changing. You have to remain observant, and
continually reevaluate whether your initial decision was correct.

Judgment is more important than ever. If there was a revolution in Chile two hundred years ago, we might not have known for
three to six months that copper prices would be affected, not until
the ship came into port and there was no copper aboard. Chile is
a copper mining country, and if somehow you could have figured
out back then that a revolution was coming, you could have made
a fortune not only in copper, but also in all the things that the
price of copper affects. The carrier pigeons arriving in London
that brought Nathan Rothschild the news of Wellington's victory
over Napoleon at Waterloo were of significant financial benefit
to Europe's famous banking family. Getting information early,
you can make a lot of money, but only if you know what to do
with it. Today we know everything instantly. And everybody has
the same information pretty much at the same time. Judgment is
what makes the difference.

If you want to make a lot of money, resist diversification. Brokers promote the notion that everybody should diversify. But that is mainly to protect themselves. If you buy ten different stocks, the chances are that some will be good. You are not going to go broke, but you are not going to make a lot of money, either. Even if you do a good job, even if seven of the stocks go up and only three go down, that is fine, but that is not going to make you rich. The way to get rich is to find what is good, focus on it, and concentrate your resources there. But make very sure you are right. Because it is also a fast way to go broke. It is why brokers tell you to diversify—to prevent your going broke and suing them.

If you want to get rich, find the few right things and invest. If in 1970 you had bought commodities and held them for ten years, and in 1980 you sold your commodities and bought Japanese stocks, and then in 1990 you sold your Japanese stocks and bought technology stocks, and then sold those in 2000, you would be fabulously rich now. But if you had diversified in 1970, and simply bought a stock average, you would not have made much money at all in those thirty years. Yes, you can diversify, and you will be safe, but you are not going to get rich. For investors who want to make a lot of money, stay with what you know, do not jump around, and invest very rarely and in a concentrated way. The downside, of course, is that if you are not as smart as you think you are, and you lose everything, you lose your shirt.

But, as I said, do not listen to me. Stay with what you, yourself, know.

. . .

THERE IS NOTHING quite like a bull market to make people think they are smart. It is remarkable how many people mistake a bull market for brains. I was lucky to have two very good employers when I started out on Wall Street. One of them was the legendary trader Roy Neuberger, who ran a firm called Neuberger Berman, where I worked briefly before moving to Arnhold and S. Bleichroeder. I remember his telling me about certain people who no longer worked for the company. They had made a lot of money for the firm, he said, but subsequently had gone on to lose fortunes, simply because they had never understood why they were making money in the first place. The reason, of course, had been the bull market of the late 1960s, spurred in part by a big mania in technology stocks. They really thought they were smart guys. They thought they deserved to make the money. But, in fact, they did not understand the market at all. They had no historical perspective, no intuitive sense of the market's ups and downs.

All big bull markets, secular bull markets, end in a bubble. Everyone chases the conventional wisdom, following what they read in the press, and that presents the smart investor with opportunities. At the same time it makes one's timing more difficult, because there are no rules in bubbles. One of the more popular books on the subject says it all in the title: *Extraordinary Popular Delusions and the Madness of Crowds*, written by Charles Mackay, first published in 1841. From the Dutch tulip mania of the seventeenth century to the South Sea Company bubble and Mississippi land scandals a century later, to the dot-com and housing bubbles of just a few years ago—all bubbles look the same.

At the time, everyone thinks what is happening is quite

rational. These prices are good, they think, and will continue to go higher. That is when my mother calls me and says she wants to invest. Everybody she knows is talking about whatever the hot thing happens to be. I ask why she wants to buy the stock, and she says: "Well, because it has tripled over the last year."

I say, "No, Mother, you don't do it that way. You don't buy it *because* it has tripled, you buy it *before* it triples."

But that is what happens in bubbles. The price goes up *because* the price is going up. In one sense, what you want in a bull market is a kid who is too young to know that what he is doing is foolish. You want a kid who will race into a bubble and leverage it higher and higher. Guys like me will not make nearly so much money because we see what is going on. The kid does not know why he is making money, which is why he is making so much money. The rest of us are experienced enough or smart enough to know that this is going to end badly. What you want is a kid with very little experience and just enough brains to be very dangerous. But you need to be smart enough to know when to pull out, to save yourself from his lack of knowledge and experience, and that, of course, can be hard to do. When things go bad, you certainly do not want that kid around—and the kid is probably not going to be around by then anyway.

Roy Neuberger was in his midtwenties when he went to work on Wall Street. He arrived in the spring of 1929, and he managed to survive the great crash in October by shorting RCA as a hedge against a decline in his blue chip stocks. In 1939, he started Neuberger Berman. He showed up at the office every day until he was ninety-nine. He was 107, and still trading, when he died in 2010.

He told me he had figured out that Wall Street was like the shoe business, which he also had been involved in at one time: You buy the shoes, you mark them up, and you sell them. You do not sit around holding the shoes for decades or even months. When a stock goes up in price, you sell it. He would buy for a day, for a week. A long-term holding for him was maybe a month or two months. He was one of the great traders on Wall Street. He became the broker for A.W. Jones.

By the time I came along A.W. Jones had been in business for twenty years, and it and Neuberger Berman were two of those firms people talked about, because both Neuberger and Jones were that much smarter than everybody else. Before working for the veteran Neuberger, I had worked for Dick Gilder, one of the new breed of young hotshots, whose firm, R. Gilder & Co., invested mainly in growth stocks. I learned a lot from both men.

As I often explain to young people, I benefited from being an assistant. I learned by watching others closely. There is nothing like on-the-job training. Many people coming into the job market think that they have done well for themselves if they manage to leapfrog an apprenticeship. The wise course is to start by working for someone else, and to keep one's eyes and ears open.

I did learn a lot from both men, but at both firms I was a fish out of water: studying growth rates all day under Dick, and following the tape minute to minute with Roy. I am an investor, not a trader. I look to buy a stock cheap and never sell it. There are plenty of ways to make money on Wall Street, and just as in any endeavor, whether it is music, art, or finance, you have to find your own way. I went out and found mine just as Roy and Dick had found theirs.

Ten years after cofounding Quantum, it was time to find my own way again.

AS EARLY AS my teenage years, dreaming of success, I had taken to telling anyone who would listen that I was going to retire at the age of thirty-five. Enjoying success on Wall Street years later, I was quite vocal about sticking to that plan. I would tell friends that I intended to have several careers, not the same career all my life. I did not want to wake up when I was seventy-five and find myself sitting on Wall Street, watching the tape. I wanted to live a variety of lives. Following that path, I might not make as much money, but there would certainly be no shortage of excitement.

One pronouncement I had persisted in making over the years, signaling to friends my desire for adventure, was that I wanted to go around the world on my motorcycle. It was one of many goals I had set for myself, and the time was now right to do it. The Roman censor Appius Claudius the Blind said, "Every man is the architect of his own fortune." And everything I had achieved up to that point in my life—along with the things I had failed at—had served to confirm that proposition. If the sentiment holds added meaning for me today, after two trips around the world, it is probably because the view is attributed to the man who built the Appian Way, the first and most famous of the ancient roads of the Roman Republic.

By 1979, I had made the decision to leave Wall Street. If only in my imagination, I had already begun to taste my freedom. But late that year the markets went through a very difficult period. At the Quantum Fund, we were pretty good at the investment game by then, and we made a lot of money, as usual. So I said no, this is too much fun, and I stayed. And so there I was. I was thirty-seven. And I had outlived my own goals. I was psychologically prepared for retirement, and would not have stayed on that much longer, but my decision to go was still not final until, suddenly, everything stopped being fun.

That year the Securities and Exchange Commission investigated us over our investment in a company called Computer Sciences Corporation. The SEC claimed that my partner, George Soros, was engaged in stock manipulation. He was charged with selling the stock short, only to cover his short sales by buying shares back at a lower price on the upcoming public offering. He was given the opportunity to sign a consent decree, in which he and the firm admitted no wrongdoing but promised not to do it again. Why would we agree to sign it? I asked him. Why sign it if we did nothing wrong? Why let it be construed that we were manipulating the stock? I was taken aback by his answer—"Because that is what I was doing," he said.

"George," I remember telling him, "my reputation is worth more to me than a million dollars."

And I remember just as clearly his answer.

"Not to me it's not," he said.

He said it jokingly, but he meant it: that making the money was more important than anything else at stake in the transaction.

Exacerbated by a series of events that started coming to my attention in the spring of 1980, the incident was the first sign that our priorities had started to diverge. I did not like what was happening. We were getting bigger. We had eight or ten employees by then. We had over a quarter of a billion dollars under management, which seemed like a lot at the time, considering that we started out with a $12 million portfolio. Things were getting more involved, and certain practices were not to my liking. I was also skeptical of certain hires, and I just did not want to take any chances like that.

All of it started coming together that spring. Nothing unusual had happened up to that time. We were just a couple of guys and a secretary. But now I could see that my reputation might come to be tarnished—or much worse. I felt the way I had felt when coxing at Oxford fifteen years earlier, after receiving that letter forwarded by my father. I was faced with a similar ethical and moral dilemma. In this case it soon became clear to me that no argument was going to change things. I tried confrontation, I raised a challenge, all to no avail. I was the junior partner. And so I said, OK, this is it. I am going to retire, as planned, and pursue a different life.

My leaving Quantum was in keeping with a family pattern of sorts. When I was a kid, my grandmother told me that one of my forebears had been a partner of American industrialist Cornelius Vanderbilt, with whom he fell out over ethics. (When I arrived at Yale as a freshman, I was assigned to Vanderbilt Hall, which was built in 1894 with money donated by Cornelius Vanderbilt II. I noticed Mr. Vanderbilt seemed to have done quite well for himself without my ancestor.) My father severed a business relationship with his older brother for similar reasons. I was operating in the same tradition, it seemed.

As I said, on Wall Street I worked all the time. I loved it that much. One Independence Day weekend—it was July the third, around seven o'clock—I received a phone call from a friend, Burton MacLean, who had been one of my classmates at Yale. Mackie worked at Brown Brothers Harriman & Co., the oldest private bank in the United States. We were the best of friends, but we had followed different paths in life. Having settled down to raise a family, he and his wife, Charlotte, had four children—unlike me, Mackie had priorities other than work.

"Why don't you come to the beach with us for the long weekend?" he said.

I said, "Oh, no, I'm working, I have some things to do."

He said, "Tomorrow's the Fourth of July, what are you talking about?"

I said, "Well, there are things to do, and they have to be done so we don't lose money."

I know he felt bad for me.

I remember, when I left Quantum, one of the first calls was from Mackie.

He said, "I heard that you retired or got fired or something."

"I retired," I said. "I don't ever have to work again for as long as I live, unless I do something wrong."

Time has a way of outrunning even the closest of friendships—all of a sudden ten years have gone by, then three times ten years—and Mackie and I have lost touch. But I still remember that call. In my mind's eye I could see him, looking out the window of his home, at his four children and his car, all of which he was still paying for, and wondering where, and at what cost, he could possibly have found the time to put in the hours that would have enabled him to retire at the age of thirty-seven. And I realized how lucky I was to have found something about which I was so passionate that I was able to pursue it to the exclusion of everything else.

5

INVESTMENT BIKER

I bought my first motorcycle in 1969, just after my arrival on Wall Street and the end of my first marriage. It was not the motorcycle on which I would circumnavigate the globe; it was a 250cc BMW and would have been sorely underpowered for the purpose. I did not make history on the bike, but on it I did participate in a significant moment in American countercultural history.

Off and on throughout the summer of 1969, I had been hearing about the "3 Days of Peace & Music" set to take place at Woodstock but was not interested enough to try to get tickets. Not until I heard reports on the radio about what was transpiring up there in the Catskills did I get excited about joining the fun. So I left work promptly on Friday, August 15, hopped on the motorcycle, and headed up to the festival. Roadblocks were up by then—the police would not let anybody get near the place—and

I drove through the backyards of various local residents to get around them. One woman came racing out of her house, screaming at me, and rightly so. Well, within three or four hundred yards I had a flat tire, so I guess she got her revenge, but I changed the flat and continued on up to the venue.

There was a fence around the stage, and I rode right up to the fence. All the security people wore green jackets with the Woodstock logo, a dove sitting on the neck of a guitar, imprinted in white on the back. And it was such a hot day that they had all hung their jackets on the fence. I crawled under the fence, got one of the jackets, put it on, and walked up to the stage. By then, of course, the place was chaos, and anybody could get away with anything if he showed any initiative at all.

And I spent the duration of the festival on the stage. I was so awed by what I had done, and so protective of what I had done—I did not want to lose my position and give up my special status—that I was very circumspect in my behavior. Periodically, people would try to climb up onto the stage, and I would say, "No, you have to stay back." I was a dutiful security man.

I had the best seat in the house. I could **see** all the action eyeball to eyeball, and on top of that I was being fed. It was terrific. At the time nobody was thinking that this was a major historical event, notwithstanding the fact that some half a million people had gathered. All we were thinking was *What a great time we're having.* We all just had our fun and went home.

The music continued through Monday, August 18, but I headed back to New York on Sunday afternoon because I had to be at work the next day. (Jimi Hendrix did not take the stage until

Monday morning, so I missed his performance.) At the office, everybody was talking about Woodstock. By then, of course, it was major news.

At one point I volunteered to my colleagues, "Oh, I was there."

They all looked at me as if I were unclean.

"What? Why would you do something like that?" they wanted to know. "Why, that's horrible."

Call it one of the earlier examples of my defying the conventional wisdom on Wall Street.

I still have my Woodstock jacket. I periodically get it out. I will show it to my children someday, though I doubt that it will mean very much to them. Maybe they will read about Woodstock. Maybe their friends will read about it—one of the girls can say, "Oh, yeah, my dad worked the security detail there."

GOING AROUND THE WORLD is hardly worthy of the expression if you have to skip China and what was then called the Soviet Union, and between my departure from Wall Street and my departure upon that adventure I spent most of my energy seeking bureaucratic approval to enter each of those countries. While waiting for permission, I went back to school.

At a party, shortly after I retired from Wall Street, I met Sandy Burton, the dean of Columbia Business School.

"Why don't you come teach a course for me?" he said.

I told him, "I don't believe business school is a particularly good thing for people, especially people who want to go into business."

I had long since taken to heart the advice I received that first

summer on Wall Street from the senior partner at Dominick &
Dominick, when he told me that attending business school would
be a waste of my time. I believed now, as he had, that there was
nothing useful to be gained by it. I had learned more about the
markets on the trading desk that summer than I would have
picked up in two years at any business school in the country.

"I really don't have any interest in teaching," I told the dean,
"and I probably wouldn't be any good at it anyway."

"Other than that," he said, with a smile, "why not come teach
a course for me?"

Two of the things I had resolved to do during my retirement
were to learn to play tennis and learn to play squash. I lived only
a few blocks from Columbia, which had an excellent gym, but
apart from students, only alumni, faculty, and staff were allowed
access to it, with the occasional exception being made, I suppose,
for those outsiders who coughed up the kind of money it took to
build a new dorm. So not long after our meeting at the party, I put
in a call to the dean.

"I'll tell you what I'll do," I said. "I will teach one course, for
one semester, for free, but what I want in return is lifetime access
to the gym."

He called me back shortly thereafter, and to my astonish-
ment, said, "OK, done."

I taught a class at the graduate school, as an adjunct professor, not knowing anything about teaching, and not having
set foot in a university myself for just about sixteen years. The
average age of the students was around twenty-six. There were
maybe fifteen of them in the class. All of them had worked for a

while. And what I said to them was this: "I am going to teach this course as if you were working for me. I am the head of research, the head of investments, at a fund, and you are going to be my analysts. I am going to give you companies to analyze, and I will teach you how to do it."

I told them how I went about analyzing companies. I gave them spreadsheets. I had the chairmen of a couple of large corporations come in, and in each case, I would sit and question the chairman as though I were a portfolio manager, an analyst, visiting him at his office, asking all the same questions I would ask if I were trying to figure out whether to invest in his company. Then I would throw it open to the students to ask questions. The assignment, after that, was to write a page, a single page—I would not accept anything longer, and I would not accept it if it were late—on what the student would do relative to that company's stock: buy it, sell it, sell it short, or do nothing.

After a few weeks of this, I had each student choose an industry to analyze—his or her choice, as long as I approved it. Say you were a student in my class and chose to be an airline analyst. We would have a dialogue in front of everybody else in the class, in which you would tell me what you thought. You would tell me how I could best make money in that industry, whether I should buy Delta, short Southwest, whatever your research told you. Everybody, I think, had three rounds. And that is the way the class worked.

I had explained that the class would be taught as a Socratic dialogue, but then had to explain to most of them who Socrates was. They all said I was a difficult taskmaster. I was very

demanding. I was also a very hard grader. I even ended up failing a guy. I said, "Listen, if I am going to put in the time coming
up here for a few hours every week, the least I expect of you is
to put in your time, too, to make it interesting for me." The students all complained, arguing that no other class was so difficult
or required them to work so hard. I was reminded of what happened to Socrates—they poisoned him. When the student evalu-
ations came out at the end of the term, I remember I was sitting
in the dean's office, expecting the worst, and when I read them,
I started crying. I got the most wonderful, glowing assessments.
Nobody had ever said such nice things about me before: "The
best course I have ever taken . . . Do whatever you have to do to
get him back . . ." I was beside myself. I had worked their asses
off, and they had appreciated it.

It had been a lot of fun, more fun than I had ever expected,
and I said to myself, all right, I will do it again. I did it for four
or five semesters. I was doing it in 1987 when the stock market
crashed. Monday, October 19. Which was my birthday. I had
been predicting a collapse, but hardly one that catastrophic. The
American market dropped over 20 percent in a day. I had been
quite vocal that the market was getting ahead of itself, that it was
really running, really heating up, and I had been insisting publicly that everyone on Wall Street would come in to work one day
to find it down 300 points. But what happened was even more
staggering. The stock market fell 512 points, the largest one-day
collapse of stocks in American history. And because, naturally, I
had shorted the market, it was, at least in one way, the best birthday I ever had.

Because everybody knew I had been predicting a crash, there was a lot of talk about me in the press. TV crews showed up at my class. A copy of one of the newspaper articles in which I was quoted was pinned to a bulletin board at the business school, and one of the other professors tore it down. He had been one of several professors teaching courses on the stock market who, in the run-up to the collapse, had been telling students, "Rogers is a fool, he does not know what he is talking about, he does not even have a PhD." He was not a happy professor.

I DO NOT believe many Americans would claim that secondary education in this country today stands as the best in the world. Indeed, most seem to agree that American primary and secondary education today is pretty hopeless. But those same people will insist, in the same paragraph, that American tertiary education is unequaled.

Maybe at one time that was true.

American universities used to be places where excellent teachers could be found, where the best of them rose to the top. But then along came tenure. It is the brass ring on the academic merry-go-round, and excellence in teaching has never been the way to attain it. Publishing and research and campus politics are what lead one to tenure. In pursuit of it, as often as not, teaching is seen as a distraction. I remember a professor once telling me, "This is a fantastic life. Too bad we have all these students around."

Tenure, at its worst, is where incompetent teachers find refuge. American academia is controlled by tenured faculty. They do research; they go to the library. Most will not say it, but students coming around, whether in need of extra help, complaining about their grades, or submitting papers that have to be graded, are an impediment to what they see as the real work of a college professor.

There is no profession in the world, *anywhere* in the world, where if you work for seven years you get a lifetime guarantee of a job. Except at a university. Becoming a doctor, becoming a partner in a law firm, you still have to produce. If you have tenure at a university, by the time you are thirty-five you never have to prove yourself again. Unless you burn down the university or murder somebody, you have a job for life. And a job as a college professor is the closest thing this side of political patronage or a mob-run construction site to a no-show job. When I was a full professor, I figured out that, averaged over a calendar year, I could fulfill my obligation by working five hours a week.

Academic tenure is a relatively recent development in American education. And the rationale behind it, academic freedom, seems a little bit ludicrous today. Does an accounting professor have to have life tenure to protect his or her political views in the classroom? A physics professor? Political beliefs about assets and liabilities? About the force of gravity on falling bodies? The professors may need protection from one another, but that is no justification for lifetime employment.

Tenure is an aspect of the exceptionalism that makes American tertiary education one of the great bubbles of our time. Right now, to go to Princeton costs $56,000 a year. That is just to get in the door: tuition and room and board. It does not include the plane fare to get there. It does not include beer. That is at least a quarter of a million dollars for a four-year course of study, and the price goes up every year. Soon it will be fifty times what it cost me to go to Yale in 1964. All the Ivy League schools, as well as Stanford and the like, have convinced everybody that admission is worth the price of the exorbitant tuition, and so far the world has fallen for the pitch, just like everybody fell for the housing bubble. There are always "good" reasons and "solid" evidence for participating in whatever the current bubble is. In three or four years, just the base cost at Princeton will be $65,000 a year.

I went to a couple of these schools, Yale and Oxford. I loved every minute of it. I had a fabulous time. It made me who I am. But if it is just an education you want, you can get a good education, if you apply yourself, at any number of places, and everyone knows this by now. What these institutions are selling today is nothing more than the sticker—the brand name, the label. And when things get tough, fewer and fewer people are going to be able to afford to pay so much for so little.

If Princeton wanted to position itself as an Asian university, yes, it could fill its classes with plenty of smart overseas students who can afford to pay their own way. Oxford, right now, could fill every class with qualified Chinese students, all of whose families would willingly, and quite easily, lay out the full fare. But an American kid who has to take out a loan to attend one of these schools faces coming out of college a couple of hundred thousand dollars in debt, and that is hardly the great future these places promise solely on the strength of their names. Loans for education cannot be written off under US bankruptcy laws. In America, if you go broke, you can write off just about everything—everything but loans you received for your education, the very debt that probably launched you on the trajectory to bankruptcy in the first place.

If the West continues to have problems, as seems likely to be the case, it is going to be extremely difficult for these places to find applicants. As expenses keep rising and institutions keep raising their prices, an increasing number of Americans will be unable to afford the tuition, while overseas students are discovering better brand names closer to home. If you look at the university rankings that have been published over the past twenty years, you will see now, for the first time, many Asian universities that were never there before: great pedigrees, great educations. There is competition coming.

And then there is technology, which to kids today is second nature. Why get up at 8:00 A.M. to drag yourself to Spanish class three days a week when you can learn more efficiently and on your own schedule via computer? Does America need thirty thousand expensive, tenured Spanish professors? Is the Spanish professor at Princeton going to teach you Spanish better than anybody else? You can learn Spanish a lot faster, probably better, and certainly for a lot less money, by going online. Likewise with accounting, physics, and calculus. What you need is a great teacher. Why not find one very talented professor, tenured or not, and let him teach the course over the web? Why not find two or three great teachers whom everybody can learn from, giving millions of students access to the best instruction available?

For some institutions of higher learning, it may already be too late. Several elite universities in the United States are now on the verge of bankruptcy. Their expense structure is unsustainable. You cannot run a business of any kind where your top people work only five hours a week, or work even ten hours a week. Do it and you are going to go bankrupt, especially operating within the constraints of a system like tenure, where it is not possible to fire anyone, not even those who, by virtue of the system, do not work very hard in the first place. Add to that the fact that Ivy League universities are traditionally overgenerous with labor, because they do not want to appear to be filthy capitalists, and bankruptcy presents itself as a blessing. We saw it with the automobile industry. The unions would come around when the contracts were up, and the auto companies would cave in. They just kept giving away the store. Eventually it bankrupted the industry.

Part of the problem is that these institutions are run by academics; they are not run by entrepreneurs. The universities are badly managed, and their endowments can no longer save them. Much of what makes up their endowments is phony. A lot of what these schools have invested in over the past twenty years has been things that are illiquid, assets for which there is no public market, whether timber or real estate or the main one, and most crippling: private equity.

In the bubble, many financial institutions carried what are known as Tier 3 assets. These are assets whose value was no more than hypothetical—mortgages, for example. Their market value was "marked to a model." If your computer program said a particular piece of paper was worth 96, you wrote down 96.

Moody's and Standard & Poor's said the paper was AAA and therefore worth 96. But we know now that most of that stuff was garbage. And it is that kind of stuff that makes up a very large share of the endowments in question.

Harvard—and this applies to all the elite schools—does not manage a lot of this money itself. A hotshot private equity guy comes in and says invest in our fund, and Harvard gives him $100 million. He goes out and invests in new ventures or buys companies; whatever he does, he marks it to model and Harvard accepts his numbers. Now the fund manager has every incentive to jack up his valuations, just as Fannie Mae and Citibank did, and just as everybody else who was using mark-to-model did. And Harvard loves to accept the numbers with pride.

All of them, in the bull market, thought they were making huge amounts of money. They spent. They gave everybody raises. Harvard went out and bought huge amounts of acreage in Boston. Yale bought a lot of acreage. They thought: *We have all this money; it is time to expand; we can be generous.* Then they all got hit with the truth—the financial meltdown—and what some of them did was start borrowing. They started selling bonds to the public, based on their respectable names and their AAA credit, and the market bought into it.

Several universities, for the first time in their histories, now have debt on their balance sheets. They have bonds they have to pay off. At the same time, many of the portfolio managers have leveraged the portfolios. They have bought things on margin. It is a classic case of how companies and institutions get into trouble. They borrow money, being told that there is no problem. Things go bad, then things get worse, and they realize that this is a permanent state, that they have a serious problem. It is especially a problem in academia because they cannot cut their expenses. They have unions, tenured professors.

Then there are the many off-the-balance-sheet obligations. One of the more absurd requires the school to pay for the college education of the children of any parent—not just a professor— who has been employed by the university for ten years. An employee with three or four children represents over $1 million of future obligations. Also, private equity deals may require an ongoing stream of funding that does not appear on the balance sheet—fine when things are going well, but troublesome when things are not and administrators need more money. Every school has millions of hidden obligations like these.

Some of the people running these university financial departments are not terribly clever. The same is true of many pension plans. Many state and city pension plans are bankrupt. In the next bear market, whenever it comes (and it will probably hit pretty soon), you are going to see more of the same. It will come as a huge shock to the world when Harvard University or Princeton or Stanford goes bankrupt, when these institutions that have been around for decades, for centuries in some cases, understand how bad their finances are.

When the big collapse came in 2008 and 2009, a lot of them were faced with having to cut back their spending. The way they traditionally operate is they take a percentage of the endowment, say 5 percent of the endowment, for running the place. But the endowment of $40 million is suddenly $24 million—as a result of the crash—and they start looking for places to make cuts. But they have already increased their expense minimums; they have taken permanent debt on their balance sheets, putting themselves in deeper trouble, and what they do then is add more debt, because they think the market will turn around. We have smart managers, they tell themselves, who assure us everything is going to be OK.

We have seen it many times. Things start spiraling downward, and by the time people start catching on, it is usually too late, as it was for Lehman Brothers and Bear Stearns. One of the advantages of this, of course, is we might get rid of tenure finally. And the Asian universities, which do not have these problems yet—gigantic salaries, gigantic union obligations, tenure obligations—will rise.

One of the more vital aspects of an American university education will survive even after the current bubble pops: the experience of going away from home to live and learn among hundreds or thousands of other eighteen- to twenty-two-year-olds. Sports teams, debating societies, social events—all will continue, even if much of academic life is conducted via a computer in a dorm room. Lecture halls might even survive, with lectures being piped in via satellite. Libraries will disappear or be converted to tennis courts.

The "creative destruction" caused by technology combined with an absurd, unsustainable cost structure will give rise to whole new centers and ways of learning—just as has happened throughout history. We have all forgotten the names of the former great world universities in places like Morocco, Timbuktu, Portugal, Italy, Asia . . . the list goes on and on.

. . .

WHILE TEACHING at Columbia, I received permission from the Chinese government to ride my motorcycle across China, a trip I made in 1988, documented by PBS as part of its *Travels* series, in an episode titled "The Long Ride." I followed it up with a five-thousand-mile journey across Pakistan and India.

When I returned home from that three-month adventure, the dean of Columbia Business School said to me, "OK, we have an offer for you."

It was an offer he described as spectacular, an offer I could not refuse. I had no idea what in the world Columbia could possibly offer that would be of any interest to me.

"What we are going to do," he said, "is make you a full professor."

In Morningside Heights and on college campuses everywhere this was very big stuff. Academicians study and lobby and fight, they spend their entire careers, angling for full professorships. I was reminded of the observation made by various people over the years, variously worded, as far back as Woodrow Wilson, and codified in the 1970s as Sayre's Law after Columbia professor and political scientist Wallace Stanley Sayre: "Academic politics are so vicious because the stakes are so low."

I took the position, but I was available to the university for only a year. I had just started teaching when word came back from Moscow granting me permission to drive across the USSR. My round-the-world trip was now possible. This was what I had been waiting for and working toward for almost a decade.

I enjoyed the time I spent at Columbia. I had a very busy life outside the school and did not socialize too much up there, but I did spend a fair amount of time trying to help students outside of class hours. At the same time that I was teaching, I was hosting a TV show, *The Profit Motive with Jim Rogers*, interviewing guests five nights a week on the Financial News Network. The first network of its kind, FNN was eventually bought by CNBC, giving that company, at least temporarily, a monopoly in the field.

A few years later I cohosted a show on CNBC called *My Portfolio* with financial journalist Bill Griffeth. This was still early in the evolution of financial programming and also early, as I experienced it, in the evolution of mobile phones. Bill and I were broadcasting live, taking calls and offering commentary, when we both were a little startled by the on-air ringing of a telephone.

"That's your phone," Bill said.

I had not thought to turn off my cell phone or, wiser yet, to leave it back in the green room before coming onto the set. If that were not sufficient to show my lack of sophistication when it came to appearing on television, what I did next pretty much sealed the deal: I answered the phone. On air.

It was my mother calling to see how I was.

"I just wanted to check up on you. I know you have been sick."

I said, "Mother, I cannot talk now, I am sitting here on TV."

Big-time broadcaster that I was.

The director of the show, much more sensible than I, cut away to a commercial. I still have people remind me of the story.

IT WAS ON my fifth bike, a 1000cc BMW R100RT, that I finally followed through on my dream to circle the world. When permission came through from the Russians, I quit both Columbia and

FNN, and along with my girlfriend, Tabitha Estabrook, who rode her own BMW, I set off on the journey in the spring of 1990.

Tabitha and I had met a couple of years earlier through an old friend of mine—her mother—and she was as adventurous as any woman I had ever known. (I had yet to meet Paige Parker.) She had traveled with me as a passenger on my motorcycle trip across Pakistan and India. A recent graduate of Amherst College, raised on the Upper West Side of Manhattan, she was just a year younger than half my age, and at the time was working as a grants administrator for a small foundation in New York.

Tabitha's father, Nick, had spent a summer when he was at Harvard touring Europe on a BMW he secretly had purchased. He never told his parents about the motorcycle he kept hidden in Europe. Yet here he was adamantly opposed to his daughter riding a motorcycle around the world. I wonder how I would react if Happy or Baby Bee ever came to me with such a preposterous suggestion.

Tabitha and I started the trip in Ireland at the end of March 1990, traveling through Europe to Central Asia, heading east from there across China, stopping in Japan before going west across Siberia into European Russia. After Poland, we returned to Ireland, then headed south through Western Europe, arriving in North Africa, and from there shot straight down the center of the continent. From South Africa we shipped our bikes to Australia, and from New Zealand we shipped them across the Pacific to Argentina, making our way through South America, Central America, and Mexico, and eventually across the United States to New York. After a stay there, we set off across the United States

and Canada to Anchorage, Alaska, eventually finishing the journey in Northern California at the home of Yale classmate Len
Baker. In all, we spent twenty-two months on the road, covering a
total of one hundred thousand miles, which put us in the *Guinness
Book of Records.* We traversed six continents and more than fifty
countries.

There is nothing like crossing outlying borders, I learned, to
get the lowdown on a country. When you cross a border, the first
thing you discover is whether you have to pay bribes. Is everything aboveboard and straightforward? Is the process efficient?
Is it a matter of ten minutes, as it should be, or does it take all
day to get through the border? You also get a sense of the local
currency, because the first thing you have to do after crossing
the border is change your money. There is always an official exchange, of course, and I always change a little bit there, because
I know the money I buy from the government is not counterfeit,
so I can use it for comparison with the money I intend to buy
on the black market. And then I find the black market, if there is
one—or, as often as not, the black market finds me.

The black market is indispensable to one's insight into a
country. Right away you know if there *is* a black market, and if so,
whether the currency carries a big premium. The black market
is like taking somebody's temperature. If I give you a thermom-
eter and we take your temperature, we know whether something
is wrong. We do not know *what* is wrong, but we do know that
something is wrong. If you have a *high* temperature, we know that
something is really wrong. The black market operates the same
way. You do not know what is wrong if there is a black market,

but it gives you the first hint. And if there is a big premium in the market—a large discrepancy between the official rate and the black market rate—you know something is seriously wrong. If you want to know something about a country, you can learn more from talking to a black marketer than from speaking to a government minister.

You drive away from the border, and you immediately know the state of the roads. Are there traffic lights? Are there proper shops, or just shacks posing as shops? Are there real hotels, or just backyard accommodations? By the time you get across the border, you know a lot about a country. And no matter how sophisticated you think you are, sometimes what you discover can come as a very big surprise.

Tabitha and I came down from Tunisia and Algeria through the center of Africa, and when we got to the Botswana border, I immediately knew—or certainly within an hour or so it became very clear—that whatever this country was, it was like nothing we had seen anywhere else in Africa. Nothing like what we had seen in a lot of places . . . Russia, Asia. No black market, no bribes, total efficiency . . . good highways, traffic lights, road signs . . . shopping centers that could have existed in any small town in America. And by the time we got to the capital, there were hotels. We had not run into anything like it in a while.

Before leaving New York, I had faced the question of what to do with my investments while I was away. Fortunately, I had been optimistic about a few sectors that did not require monitoring on a daily basis, so most of my assets were in utility stocks, government bonds, and foreign currencies, and in anticipation of the trip

I pretty much left the money where it was. I would enjoy gains if I was right, and I would not get wiped out if I was wrong. I cut back on my shorts and kept no futures positions at all. This was not an investment trip, but whenever I travel, being who I am, I am alert to promising opportunities. In Botswana I knew there was a stock market, and I immediately started investing. I bought every share on the exchange.

Lest you think I am a big hitter, there were only seven companies listed on the Botswana stock exchange at the time. I kept them until five or six years ago. Whenever there was a new issue or a stock dividend, I would buy more. Botswana is a very big country with a small population, but it had the good sense to possess one of the largest diamond mines in the world. I continued to reinvest everything in Botswana until around 2007 or 2008 when I decided to sell all my emerging markets because they were all being overexploited. There were twenty thousand MBAs flying around the world, looking for the new hot market. So I sold Botswana, after eighteen years of great gains.

Tabitha and I returned from the final leg of the trip in the late summer of 1992. By the time I finished writing *Investment Biker*, my book about the adventure, Tabitha had set off for graduate school to earn a degree in international relations, a subject she was by then probably better equipped to teach than were those professors of hers who had studied it only in classrooms. What has become of her since I do not know.

6

THE RISE OF COMMODITIES

At a speaking engagement to promote *Investment Biker* at the Mint Museum in Charlotte, North Carolina, I met the woman who would become the mother of my children. Her name was Paige Parker. She was from Rocky Mount, about two hundred miles northeast of Charlotte, and as lovely, to my way of thinking, as anything to come out of that city since the music of native son Thelonius Monk. She was twenty-seven years old and working as a fund-raiser for Queens College of Charlotte. She had read *Investment Biker* on the recommendation of the college president, who told her I was going to be making an appearance in town and suggested she attend.

I was walking into the auditorium to speak, and there she was, standing in the doorway. We started talking. She said things like: "Oh, you're better looking in person than you are on TV."

She had never seen me on TV. Things like: "I've always wanted to drive across the United States." When I asked, "What's stopping you?" she answered, "I can't afford it now because I don't have the necessary *cash flow*, . . ." using all the right terminology. When I got home the next day, I called her.

"Come to New York this weekend," I said, "and go to the ballet."

"I won't stay at your place," she said. "I'll stay in a hotel."

She had been to New York a few times, knew that it was expensive and that most Manhattanites lived in small apartments, so when I told her my place was large enough that we would not run into each other during her brief stay, she thought I was mad or certainly misleading her. She insisted on a hotel, for which she would pay.

I said, "Fine."

We went to the ballet in the afternoon, the Paris Opera Ballet's performance of *La Bayadère*. I was keen on dance, and to my delight, Paige loved it too, since she had been dancing most of her life. From Lincoln Center we walked about forty blocks up Broadway to my town house on Riverside Drive, overlooking the Hudson. There I rolled out my bicycle built for two and we rode to Central Park for dinner at the Boathouse café. I told her I was planning to go to the Henley Regatta and asked her to come with me. She accepted the invitation, we attended the regatta together a few weeks later, and the rest is history. If you do not fall in love at the Henley Regatta—sitting there in the sun on deck chairs, drinking champagne, eating strawberries with clotted cream—you are not going to fall in love.

We had been dating for a little over a year when she quit her job in Charlotte and moved to New York. She took her own apartment there in the fall of 1997 and started work as a director at a marketing firm. By then I was totally hooked. A year later I asked her to be my wife. By now, plans were under way for what would be our three-year Millennium Adventure, in which we would circumnavigate the planet by car—a custom-built, four-wheel-drive convertible Mercedes—covering half again the distance of my motorcycle trip. I wanted to capitalize on a historic moment, to take the world's pulse at the end of one millennium and the start of another. We were in no position to specify wedding plans— who knew where we would be or where we would want to be at the time—but we did set a date for the ceremony: January 1, 2000.

We started the trip in Iceland on January 1, 1999, and drove through 116 countries, some of them seldom visited: Saudi Arabia, Myanmar, Angola, Sudan, Congo, East Timor, and the like. We traveled through jungles, deserts, war zones, epidemics, and blizzards. We camped with nomads and camels in the Sahara and swilled beer in the barren wastes of Siberia with Russian workingmen and mobsters. With sixty million Hindus in Allahabad, India, we washed away our sins in the Ganges at the historic Maha (Great) Kumbh Mela, which happens every 144 years. I ate silkworms, iguanas, snakes, termites, guinea pigs, porcupines, crocodiles, and grasshoppers. It was not only a great adventure, but also part of the continuing education that I had been engaged in all my life.

This time I traveled down the west coast and up the east coast of Africa, visiting over thirty countries there. We traveled from Africa across Arabia and the Indian subcontinent to

Indochina, Malaysia, and Indonesia. The trip took us through approximately half of the world's thirty civil wars. Paige ended up planning the wedding by cell phone and e-mail over a period of months, while driving across Siberia and through parts of Mongolia and various countries in Europe. We were married at the turn of the millennium in a storybook ceremony—a carriage, white horses—at Henley-on-Thames, where we had fallen in love three and a half years earlier. We arrived back in New York on January 5, 2002, after covering 152,000 miles and setting another Guinness record, for the longest continuous car journey.

Throughout the trip, whenever we stopped, whether in Africa or Siberia or the United States, wherever we traveled, our custom-crafted, hybrid, bright yellow Mercedes attracted attention. In Palo Alto, California, toward the end of our journey, after dinner at Spago (Wolfgang Puck closed his restaurant there in 2007), we struck up a conversation with a guy who was standing outside, looking the car over. When we explained to him what we were doing, he said: "You're living everyone's dream."

The glamour and excitement of traveling the world was a fantasy shared by numerous people we had encountered over the preceding three years. In fact, an independent poll coincidentally taken after we returned showed the number one dream held by people around the world was to chuck it all, get in the car, and drive around the world.

"I've always wanted to do this," he said.

He had recently made some money, he told us, thanks to the dot-com boom, and now he felt he could finally afford to follow through on his wish. I encouraged him to do so.

"That's a two-seater," he said, with a curious look in his eye. "Do you mean that the two of you sat side by side all that time?"

The odometer at the time was showing 145,000 miles.

"Yes," I said.

"Three years? And you're still together?"

He was incredulous. He and his fiancée had set out on a five-day coast-to-coast trip, he said, and before they reached their destination the engagement was off.

"I got out of the car in Denver, and she didn't even slow down."

BEFORE PAIGE AND I set off around the world, I started the Rogers International Commodity Index.

By the end of the 1990s, I had come to the conclusion that the bear market in commodities was coming to an end. It was a topic I had been pressing pretty consistently in media appearances, which had become a regular part of my life since the publication of *Investment Biker*. I saw the commodities bull market coming, but to invest in commodities while I was traveling would have been close to impossible. With commodities you have to stay on top of everything all the time. Commodities contracts expire. Who knew if I would have access to them? I decided that the solution was an index fund, and in order to invest, I would have to start my own. There were no commodities index funds at the time. Commodities were still a widely neglected and unknown sector.

Throughout my investing career, I had invested in stocks and bonds, currencies and commodities, all over the world, on both the long side and the short side. When I first started reading the commodities page in the *Wall Street Journal*, it consisted of a single page, but even back then I considered it important. Looking through my library, I see that my first copy of the *Commodity Research Bureau (CRB) Yearbook* is dated 1971. So at least that early, somewhere between 1968, when I began my first full-time Wall Street job, and the day I received that book, I was curious enough to seek out the principal source of information on the subject.

In those days, of course, while I was successfully investing in them, most other people paid no attention to commodities at all. Maybe part of the problem—or part of my success—was that I did not know enough to understand that I should actually be ignoring them. Had I gone to business school, I would have known that commodities were not important and would have paid them little regard, but I did not go to business school and did not come up through a proper investment-bank training program.

As mentioned, we took a big hit in stocks at Quantum when President Richard Nixon closed the gold window in August 1971. When he reopened it, three years later, we made a big score in commodities. A year before resigning his office, Nixon, in response to worldwide outrage, restored convertibility between the US dollar and gold for US citizens, which Franklin Roosevelt had ended in 1933 despite his earlier promises not to do so. Gold at the time was pegged on the world market at $35 an ounce. By the first day of trading on which Americans could buy it, January 1, 1974, the price of gold, in anticipation of a run on it, had shot up 600 percent, to $200 an ounce.

Merrill Lynch showed up that day on the floor of the London Gold Fixing, ready to buy for its American clients. Our fund sold them the gold. We shorted the gold to them, because we knew enough about markets to understand that everybody was running ahead of the approaching big buyer. The price had gone up too high too fast. Merrill Lynch was stocking up in anticipation of the big buy. It is a time-honored principle—but most people, for some reason, seem not to be aware of it—that whenever the market knows that somebody is coming, the market rises accordingly. Markets are very smart; they always run ahead. So gold, over the next several months, went down to $100 an ounce, losing 50 percent of its value, and we realized substantial gains.

But even $100 was a far cry from $35. In 1974, gold production had been static for almost half a century. With the price of gold set internationally (first at $20, then $35), it was not worthwhile for a gold miner to dig. Unless he had access to some vast mother lode, he was not going to make very much money—the price was not going to go up. But with the rise in demand and skyrocketing prices, production eventually expanded. Miners are not dumb. *That gold I discovered back in 1966*, the miner might say to himself, *was not worth extracting when gold sold for $35 an ounce, but now at $100 and rising, it's time to reopen the mine.*

Six years later, in the spring of 1980, because the fundamentals were indeed very sound—supply was low, the US dollar was being debased, the country was smothered in debt and was running a serious balance of trade deficit—gold reached $850 an ounce.

The bull market in raw materials had lasted over fifteen years. Prices went up and production came in, and as the supply increased, exceeding demand, the prices of gold and other commodities went back down. And prices stayed down for almost another twenty years. One of the more visible drops was in the energy sector. The price of oil went up over 1,000 percent in the 1970s. And then oil discoveries started coming to market. North Sea oil started flowing. Alaskan and Mexican oil started reaching the market. And at the same time, the world, in its wisdom, started cutting back on consumption. Jimmy Carter appeared on television sitting by the fire wearing a sweater. Thermostats were turned down. Small cars started appearing all over the world. Demand slowed, the supply increased, and oil went down for eighteen or nineteen years. The bear market in raw materials lasted through the 1990s.

It is classic economics. The cure for high prices is high prices. It always works.

The truth is that commodities are actually simpler to figure out than stocks. Nobody can understand IBM, not even the chairman. IBM has hundreds of thousands of factors—employees, products, parts, suppliers, competitors, governments, balance sheets, and unions—that it has to deal with. Cotton, by contrast, is pretty straightforward. All you have to know about cotton is this: Is there too much cotton or too little cotton? Cotton does not care who the chairman of the Federal Reserve is. The head of IBM has to know and care about such things. Cotton: Is there too much or too little? Now, figuring that out may not be easy at all, but the question itself is simple, and in the end it is the only question with which you have to be concerned.

To start a commodities fund I had to start my own index. There were other indexes out there, but I could not put my money into them since they were badly constructed. The others were very narrow. For example, the Goldman Sachs Commodity Index was about two-thirds energy. What kind of index is that? You might as well invest in oil. More important, they changed the index every year. One year, livestock, for example, was weighted at 26 percent; a few years later it was weighted at 4 percent. You had no way of knowing what you were going to own in three or four years. And neither did Goldman Sachs. And it was my money I was investing, not my clients' money. Goldman Sachs arbitraged extensively against its own customers. I had no customers. I wanted something that would make money for me, and any clients who invested with me

The Dow Jones Commodity Index, likewise, changed all the time. And there you could find things like aluminum weighted more heavily than wheat. There were people in the world who had never even seen, much less used, aluminum. But everybody relied on wheat. The Reuters/Jefferies CRB Index, which I also looked at, had orange juice and crude oil weighted equally. Another problem with all the indexes was their geographic myopia. Most of them reflected only what was going on in the time zones in which they operated. They restricted themselves to things that traded in London and the United States. I did not know how anyone could have invested seriously using any of them. You could not even call it gambling—with gambling, you at least know how many cards are in the deck.

I started my index on August 1, 1998, which, when I look back, I find pretty astonishing in terms of timing. It happened to be within four to six months of the bottom of the nineteen-year bear market. I am not very good at market timing, I am not very good at short-term trading, but this is one calculation that I got exactly right. Whatever success I have had investing I attribute to my remaining alert to major changes and trends developing, and as I said, I have learned enough about myself to know that I am usually a year or two, maybe three years, early. This was a notable exception.

The commodities bear market was over, and a bull market was about to begin. The Rogers International Commodity Index was a broad-based vehicle for consistent investment in raw materials, calculated from some thirty-six commodities from thirteen international exchanges. From the outset it has had higher compound returns than other commodity indexes. As of August 2012, RICI had returned a total of 281 percent. The S&P over the same period showed a total return of 62 percent.

WHILE PAIGE AND I were driving around the world I got calls that an economist at Goldman Sachs, Jim O'Neill, had coined the term "BRIC." In a paper published in 2001, he predicted a shift in global power away from G7 countries to the developing world, specifically Brazil, Russia, India, and China, hence the acronym. These four countries, all of which Paige and I would actually traverse, comprise one quarter of the world's landmass and 40 percent of its population, and according to O'Neill, their combined economies by the middle of the century would eclipse the combined economies of the world's richest nations. Of course, he had no idea what he was talking about, and as I have pointed out to him since, speaking to him face-to-face as recently as the year of this writing, clinging to the thesis shows an ignorance of the world that is disconcerting, at best. But backing off the proposition is more than he can do. It is the hobbyhorse that has carried him to the celebrity he enjoys, and he shows no signs of dismounting before riding it into the ground.

Picking China to succeed—it was the one country out of the four O'Neill had even bothered to visit—did not make him smart. The country's economic ascendancy, by then, was lighting up everybody's radar screen. I had been writing and broadcasting about it for more than ten years, since first crossing the country by motorcycle in 1988.

O'Neill's ignorance of Brazilian history has led him, today, to disregard the fact that the country owes its prosperity almost exclusively to the bull market in commodities, which like all bull markets will come to an end. Restrictions on foreign ownership of land, exchange controls, the imposition of high tariffs, and rising protectionism—the foolishness that politicians inevitably get up to—all bode ill for Brazil's productivity in the future. The Brazilian people themselves have a saying: "Brazil is the next great country in the world. It always has been and it always will be." The reason it is destined never to vindicate its promise, they say, is that, while "Brazil is God's chosen country, the one country He loves the best, the problem is that He sent Brazilians to run it."

Any uptick in Russia's fortunes derives from the same commodities bull market that is casting sunshine on Brazil, and it will be just as temporary. Russians are currently facing the worst of all worlds. With a very low birthrate, their demographic problem is quite serious—the population is rapidly aging—and the rising number of people leaving the country further exacerbates it. The problem would be even worse if so many ethnic Russians, unwelcome where they live in the states of the former Soviet socialist republics, were not being forced to return to Russia. Add to its predicament a low life expectancy in Russia, compared with that in other countries, and it is hard to see how O'Neill's hypothesis ever gained any traction. In my view, Russia, which is already something of a basket case, will continue to disintegrate. Many of the outlying areas of Russia, with different ethnic groups, religions, and languages, have secession movements. I am certainly optimistic about the changed attitude of Moscow, but one must keep perspective.

By contrast, the high birthrate in India may cause more problems than it solves. It is projected that soon the population of India will exceed that of China, a country about three times its size. And India is not capable of feeding all those people. It has already proved incapable of feeding the people it has. India should be one of the more agriculturally productive countries in the world, but government policy prevents that from happening. Indian farmers can own no more than five hectares, or about twelve acres, of land, so mass production and economies of scale are close to impossible. The infrastructure in many agricultural areas has been neglected or is nonexistent, so crops, even in bumper years, spoil before they get to market. The country is hopelessly bound up in bureaucracy as stifling as any in the world, and the government is both corrupt and chronically inept.

India, as we see it on a map, is not a rational construct. It never existed as we see it today until 1947. It was something the

English threw together in their panic to get out of there in the waning days of the Raj. The English jury-rigged India's borders, corralling numerous ethnic groups—with numerous languages and numerous religions—and very few of them get along. It is a country with a Muslim minority but is still, as home to a billion people, one of the larger Muslim countries in the world. And the Muslims and majority Hindus continue to slaughter one another.

And yet, in 1947, when it achieved its independence, India was one of the more successful countries in the world, a democratic country. But despite democracy, or maybe because of it, India has never lived up to its potential. China was a shambles as recently as 1980. India was far ahead of it. But since then China has left India, literally, in the dust. China opened its borders and its economy to the rest of the world. Walmart has stores all over China. In protectionist India, foreigners cannot open stores; doing so has been seen as a national security threat. As China rises, India continues to decline relatively. Its debt-to-GDP ratio is now up to 90 percent, making a strong growth rate virtually impossible.

Jim O'Neill, when celebrating its virtues, had never been to India, much less spent two and a half months crisscrossing it by car, as Paige and I were doing that year. He was not alone in being clueless. "Global affairs expert" Stephen Roach, Morgan Stanley's chairman for Asia, went to India for the first time in 2004, and he returned home glowing. He recounted his visit to the Taj Mahal, which is located in the city of Agra (and is an experience not to be missed), and he described a variety of mishaps along the road, blaming them for the fact that the drive from Delhi took an extraordinary five hours. The trip is only 200 kilometers, about 120 miles. What Stephen did not know about India, and was unlikely to discover on a three-day visit, was that it *always* takes five hours to get from Delhi to Agra. And that is when things go right. But that is the level of sophistication that passes for wisdom on Wall Street.

By 2001, everybody on Wall Street knew at least one person from India, because Indians were running their derivatives departments. I remember in the late 1990s having lunch with a pair of high-level executives from two different firms, talking about all the things going on in their trading departments, and they were starting to talk about derivatives. One of them said to the other, "Well, how do we get into this?" And the other guy said, "Get yourself an Indian."

India has very few universities, certainly very few for the size of the population, so Indians, if they are ambitious, have to go abroad to get educated, and great numbers of them come to the United States to get degrees. Known for their focus on math and engineering, many are interested in finance, and back then they ended up in the trading rooms, back offices, and money management departments of New York financial firms, using their math skills to create the derivatives with which Wall Street at the time was striking up a romance.

So by 2001, largely because of the position of Indians on everyone's table of organization, the not-so-smart people on Wall Street took to thinking that something was happening in India. Jim O'Neill assumed that the country had to be one of those rising stars like China. He pulled out a map and saw that the two countries were next to each other. Hmm. Both were big, both were populous—which was true of both Brazil and Russia, too, now that he thought of it—but after that, it is clear, he did not have a clue, any more than Stephen Roach, who without ever having visited India was named Morgan Stanley's chairman for Asia. But give credit where credit is due. (B)razil, (R)ussia, (I)ndia, (C)hina . . . O'Neill was off by only three letters.

(I should add that while I sometimes disagree with these guys, I continue to like them both. My comments are more a reflection of what passes for "international knowledge" in the investment world.)

7

HOME ON THE HUDSON

The Millennium Adventure is the subject of my second book, *Adventure Capitalist*.

In New York, seventeen months after we returned home from that trip—the first eight of which were spent waiting for the many vaccines we had taken to clear our systems—Paige gave birth to our daughter Hilton Augusta Parker Rogers, who would later nickname herself Happy, and I became a father for the first time. Before my second daughter, Beeland Anderson Parker Rogers, nicknamed Baby Bee, was born, Paige and I had started making plans to sell our house in New York and move to Asia.

The house I owned in New York was a house I had lived in for thirty years. I bought it in 1976. When I was working on Wall Street and living in the Manhattan apartment that Lois had rented for us when we were married, while Lois was studying at Columbia and I was stationed at Fort Hamilton, I never really took to apartment living. In the years since our divorce I had been scouring real estate ads in the newspaper and spent weekends traveling the city and the tristate area on my motorcycle in search of a house. The apartment was on Riverside Drive, and I really liked the location. Riverside Drive not only bordered the Hudson but was situated park-side as well. I cruised all five boroughs, as well as parts of New Jersey and Connecticut, looking for a house overlooking the water and/or fronting some open space. I hardly expected to find both, and never guessed that if I were to find such a house, I would find it right next door.

I was bicycling along Riverside Drive one day in late 1976, and the woman with whom I was bicycling, knowing that I was looking to move, pointed to a five-story building we passed, and said, "That house looks empty." The building was not a house, but two town houses, attached, and there was yard space on both sides of the property, north and south. The house on the downtown side bordered a building that also had a yard, so there was about forty feet of open space on the south side of the property. The place was big, it was imposing, it was beautiful, and it *was* empty. At City Hall I looked up the property's ownership and sent a letter to the owner with a self-addressed postcard enclosed, asking if the building was for sale and expressing my interest in buying it.

The property belonged to the Catholic Church. It had been part of the former Woodstock College, the oldest Jesuit seminary in the United States, which had moved to Manhattan from rural Woodstock, Maryland, in 1969 and finally, due to financial difficulties—as well as the loss of seminarians to the lure of the swinging New York City of the time—had closed in 1974. Since that time the church had been looking to sell it. The church's difficulty in doing so stemmed in part from the fact that while the north half of the building had been converted to apartments sometime in the 1930s, the south half was still configured as a single-family house, the purpose for which it had been built in 1899, when New York was booming and there was a healthy market for real estate featuring ten thousand feet of living space. The church felt it could never sell that house unless it was sold as part of a package deal.

It was the south house I had my eye on, and I worried about buying the property and then not finding a buyer for the north half. Renovating ten apartments in a huge building was not something I had the time or the energy or the know-how to do. I was down on Wall Street running a hedge fund, working fifteen hours a day every day, and while I could have made money renting or selling the apartments, in the end it would have been a bad use of my time. I talked to Donald Porter, a friend in the real estate business, told him about this splendid structure, and after looking at it, he agreed to buy the north half of the property. Inflation was rampant at the time, real estate was collapsing around the country, interest rates were skyrocketing, and long-term mortgages were hard to get—the church was so excited to sell the property that it offered us a thirty-year mortgage at a very low rate. Donald immediately started renovating and eventually sold the apartments as co-ops. I moved into the south house.

My plan was to camp out in the house for a while, to see how

I would live in the place before renovating and furnishing it. Still working on Wall Street, still frantically trying to get ahead in life, I had very little time on my hands, and I had never occupied so vast a space. I had been living in a one-bedroom apartment, I had no furniture to speak of, and I was looking at five floors and ten thousand square feet of completely empty, turn-of-the-century mansion.

I remember, after buying the house, going up to look at it at night. I had to take a flashlight along, because the place was so dimly lit. I recall going around the corner to the hardware store, after closing on the property, and buying $200 worth of lightbulbs. The storeowner had never seen anything like it. In 1977, $200 bought a lot of lightbulbs, and it took that many to light up the house in just the most basic way. One night I took a girlfriend and a few of her friends along with me, and one of her friends made the following observation: "Mardi Gras is coming, you have this big empty house, and it's perfect for a Mardi Gras ball."

We put together a group called the South House Krewe, which consisted mainly of the people who had been there that night—three journalists, a lawyer, a Columbia professor, a banker, and two of us from Wall Street—and held a Mardi Gras costume ball. The ball would become an annual affair and pretty well known in New York. Each of us was allowed a limited number of invitees, and we sent out fancy invitations. Over the years, as might be expected, word about the party built, and mobs of people made a habit of showing up uninvited. We did not turn people away. It would have been impractical and inhospitable to do so. It was like Woodstock that way.

The Jesuits had used what would eventually be the living room as a chapel. There was an altar where one of the house's eight fireplaces had been. You walked up a magnificent stairway, and on the left was a large dining room—the middle room on that floor—and to the right, closed off by heavy mahogany doors, was the chapel, its altar still in position but no longer attached to the wall. (Eventually I had the fireplace reopened and a mantel installed.) We removed the doors, opened the space up, and that is where the ball took place, with the band playing there in the living room. In the dining room we set up the bar.

We hosted the annual ball for six years running, because for six years I had never gotten around to fixing the place up enough. Once renovation and decorating had progressed to a point where hosting such a party became impractical, we stopped throwing it. I received several calls the day on which the ball would have been held that year, asking, "What time will the party start?" The original Krewe gathered for a private black-tie dinner at my house that night, throughout which the doorbell kept ringing with people in costume at the door.

By 1982, two years after I retired, I was ready to renovate. There was beautiful woodwork throughout the house, chiefly mahogany and oak, and I hired a crew to set about restoring it. In some cases that meant having first to strip the wood of paint. The Jesuits had not been interested in the house's esthetics; they concentrated on getting to heaven, not re-creating it in this world. They did take excellent care of the infrastructure. The construction was sound, and all the pipes and wiring were in very good shape. The place needed merely to be cleaned up and shined. I hired both an architect and an interior decorator, and with the latter I started furnishing the ten bedrooms, some of which I converted to other uses, creating a library and billiard room, among other things. I had the elevator, which ran to the fifth floor, extended to the roof, and put a deck up there, where I installed a hot tub, a steam bath, and an outdoor kitchen, creating an extra living space, a recreation area for the most part. I built a barbecue pit in the backyard. The food critic for the *New York Post*, who visited once, said it was the only built-in barbecue she had seen in Manhattan in her career.

I was turning the place into my home in the country. I had everything I wanted. Once a couple visited with their children, and after three or four hours that afternoon their little boy asked, "When are we going back to New York?" His family lived in an apartment, and everybody he knew lived in an apartment. He thought he had left the city. And he was right there on Riverside Drive. I doubt that I will ever find such a perfect place again.

RETURNING FROM our Millennium Adventure, Paige and I were that much more certain that China was the world's next great nation. I had been writing about it and lecturing about it since my first trip across China, and for years I had been recommending to viewers, whenever I appeared on television, that they teach their children Mandarin. So now, the father of a child myself, it was time to take my own advice.

Not speaking a foreign language fluently had always made me feel inadequate, especially given that I was an international investor and had gone on to become a worldwide traveler. Visiting many strange places, I knew that I was missing great opportunities, appreciating what was going on only through an interpreter. We all know how much gets lost in translation. The limitation was very real to me, and just like all parents trying to make up for their own inadequacies or certain things that they missed in life, it was very important to me that any children of mine not start their lives with such a disadvantage.

I had taken two years of French at Demopolis High School. At Yale, I had to satisfy a language requirement, and when I arrived, I was put into a class with students who similarly had studied French for two years. The class was conducted entirely in French—by a Frenchman, as it happened—and I never had a clue what was going on. As I mentioned, I felt very insecure at Yale. All these guys were better educated than I, with better backgrounds; many had gone to prep school, and a large number of them were from affluent areas of the country. I always felt a bit behind the curve. So that experience made my view on a foreign-language education even more significant.

As a traveler I had seen the advantages of automatically knowing a language and speaking it like a native—that is, speaking it instinctively, and with no accent. Experience in foreign countries had convinced me that a convicted felon, if he spoke the language well, could be standing next to a PhD, a multimillionaire, or a diplomat who did not speak as fluently, and the convict would receive more attention and be afforded more credibility by his audience than the other three, who in conversation would be inevitably marginalized. I was adamant that my children not just be proficient in a foreign language, but that they speak it like natives.

Now for all I know, my girls might wind up moving to Bolivia and never use their Mandarin as long as they live. Being bilingual will not make them successful in and of itself. There are dishwashers who speak Mandarin and English who are not terribly successful. I have met hundreds of people who are perfectly bilingual who are not successful at all. What I do know is that it is a skill that many people—including me—do not have, and that to smart, motivated, persistent people it will be a great advantage. Had I thought that Brazil was going to be the most important country in the future, chances are we would have started them off with Portuguese, and we might be living in South America now.

In New York we hired Shirley Ni, a Mandarin-speaking Chinese governess for Happy, and in 2006 we enrolled Happy in St. Hilda's & St. Hugh's, the only school in Manhattan that taught Mandarin to three-year-olds. The children there spoke the language only one hour a week. It was a start, but it soon became clear that it was going to take more than that. I had run into many Chinese people in the United States who spoke Mandarin to their children, but by the age of eight or nine, the children had taken to responding exclusively in English. Everyone at school, all their friends, spoke English—speaking Mandarin was not cool. Like all children, they were determined to go their own way. One day Happy, who was two or three at the time, came home from the park and said, "I want to speak Spanish." As it happened, in Riverside Park, Spanish was common. All the nannies were Puerto Rican or Central American, so all the children were conversing in Spanish, and Happy felt as though she did not belong, "because I speak Chinese."

It was clear that Happy, growing up in New York, would never continue speaking Mandarin like a native. If we were serious about her becoming totally fluent in the language, we decided, we really would have to bring her up where she had no choice but to speak it in order to communicate. Somewhere where she could not just suddenly say, "I am not going to speak Chinese." Obviously, one could not do that in a Chinese-speaking city. The decision coincided with what I saw as a serious period of decline in America—the debt hurtling out of control, an irresponsible foreign policy, and the lack in the city of New York itself of any fiscal discipline or control. Living in the city would not be terribly pleasant in the future. With all these things coming together, it made a lot of sense to uproot the family and offer our children something else. So we put the house up for sale and started looking for a place to live in Asia. I had previously ridiculed parents for relocating to benefit their kids; now I was doing it too.

8

THE LARGEST DEBTOR
NATION IN HISTORY

When Paige and I sold the house, I suffered a serious case of seller's remorse. I knew I would never live in such a wonderful house again. There are very few like it in existence. I kept thinking: *I have just sold Happy's birthright. I am selling her birthright out from under her. She will never get to live in this house.* I put a clause in the sales agreement giving me the right of first refusal on the property, if the buyers ever decided to sell it. The opportunity to buy it back made putting it on the market less painful.

At the time, 2007, I was very vocal about a housing bubble. I had seen real estate going up steadily for the three decades that I had owned the house, and I was convinced that the market had peaked. I was short homebuilding stocks. I was short Fannie Mae. Appearing on television every week, I was publicly predicting a crash.

"Can you keep your mouth shut about real estate?" Paige said. "Can you just stop talking about a housing bubble every time you talk to the press? We are trying to sell this house!"

We sold at the peak of the market. The crash came shortly thereafter. And today, if the owners called and offered to sell me the house, it would probably be at a lower price than they paid for it. But now there is no way I would buy it. I simply cannot conceive of living in New York again. We travel to the United States at least once a year, mainly to see Paige's parents and to see my mother, who is now in her nineties. We take the opportunity to visit friends in New York, and while there we stay in hotels. New York had always been my favorite city in the world, and it remains one of my favorite cities, but as much as I love New York, I cannot overlook the obvious.

Having lived in Asia for a few years now, I can tell you that when you fly into a New York airport, you are flying into a third world airport. Then you get into a third world taxi, you ride on third world highways, and even if you stay in a five-star hotel, you are staying in a third world five-star hotel. Five-star hotels in New York do not compare to five-star hotels in Asia. Nothing does . . . the infrastructure, the transportation. New York does not work anymore. JFK is just an embarrassment now. Go to Shanghai or Hong Kong or Singapore, and you are in a different world, a vibrant world.

Make no mistake, the East, specifically China, is going to experience plenty of problems, as societies always do in the rise to power and glory. When America was rising to power, it survived major setbacks, enduring civil war, several economic depressions, human rights abuses, a breakdown in the rule of law, massacres, and political corruption. In nineteenth-century America, most people could not even vote; there were few civil rights, and you could buy and sell congressmen. You can still buy and sell congressmen, but in those days they were cheaper. Back then you could buy four or five for what it costs to buy one of them today. In 1907, the whole system collapsed, just as the United States was about to become the most successful country of the twentieth century. So China will have its setbacks. But the trajectory is nonetheless clear.

There is a palpable excitement being in Asia. Step outdoors and you feel you are part of a place that is heading forward. There is a throb in Asia, a dynamism that no longer exists in America, the same feeling I used to have in New York but do not get from New York anymore. Not everywhere in Asia, obviously—I do not get that feeling in Delhi. But go to a place like Hong Kong, go into restaurants there, walk down the street, and you get the fabulous feeling that *this* is where it is. You might have that feeling in New York at times, but not as you do in Asia, where the feeling is all-pervasive.

New York is the economic and cultural capital of what is now the largest debtor nation in the world, the largest debtor nation in the *history* of the world. The world's largest creditor nations are in Asia. That is where the assets are. That is where the dynamism and energy are: China, Japan, Taiwan, Korea, Singapore, Hong Kong. Their rate of savings and investing is high. China's, at the time of this writing, is over 30 percent. Singapore's, through the 1980s, was more than 40 percent, helping to make Singapore the great success story that it is. Even Karl Marx understood that without capital, savings, and investing, it is very difficult to develop your economy. (His assumption that the country would grow and that the people would be better-off if the *state* accumulated and invested the capital is where he was proved to be totally wrong. He was right about developing capital.) America's savings rate, currently 4 percent, hovered around 2 percent for most of the past decade and actually went negative a couple of times. We are using up our capital at a rapid pace, following the path of Britain after the First World War.

As recently as 1987 the United States was a creditor nation. In 1945, coming out of the Second World War, the one country still on its feet, we were the world's largest foreign creditor. In the course of a mere three generations, we have become its largest debtor, and little can save us from bankruptcy. America came out of the Second World War with large debts to pay, but also with access to staggering amounts of accumulated capital, money that Americans were unable to spend during the war and the Great Depression, money they were by circumstances forced to save. For fifteen years demand had been pent up and building. America had the excess industrial capacity after the war to meet it, and, thanks to high personal and corporate savings, which continued into the mid-1960s, America had the healthy bank balances to pay for it. Americans started spending their savings, which led to greater investment, a growing economy, and a long period of great prosperity, during which the nation was able to pay off its debts. Today America faces overwhelming debt and no savings with which to fight it.

At the end of the nineteenth century, up until 1914, America was a debtor nation. It had borrowed a lot of money to get where it was. But the money went into canals, factories, railroads, and the like. There is nothing wrong with borrowing money as long as you invest it wisely, or as long as you have other assets. As a creditor, eventually, the United States started paying off those debts and emerged as the most successful country in the twentieth century, reaping the rewards of its sound investment. Today America is borrowing money to pay for military hardware that sits and rusts in the sun. The man who manufactures the hardware makes money, but after that, there is no beneficiary. The investment does not represent an ongoing source of production, the way a canal or a railroad does. Today we spend our borrowed money on transfer payments (over 60 percent of all government spending and more than all government revenue), and the people who get the payments certainly have a wonderful time, but such payments do nothing for future productivity. If, as a nation, you are just consuming, instead of investing and saving, the borrowed money does you little good.

What is worse, the people we have entrusted with the responsibility for addressing the problem—too much consumption, too much debt—have decided that the solution lies in yet more consumption and more debt.

THE PEOPLE WHO brought you the crash of 2008 are still holding forth. And lest you be tempted to attribute my low opinion of them to some sort of bitterness—a response to a decline in my portfolio, perhaps—let me remind you that by the time of the crash, precipitated by the burst of the housing bubble, I had most of my money out of equities, with the following exceptions: I was *short* Citibank, all the investment banks, the homebuilders, and Fannie Mae. The incompetence in Washington and on Wall Street was in fact good to people like me. While countless Americans were watching their life savings evaporate, the skeptical investor enjoyed significant gains. (As did many of the incompetent bailed-out bankers who helped Americans blow their life savings, one of those shameless inequities for which you can also thank your representatives in Washington.)

Incompetence is something you can always count on from politicians and bureaucrats. For years now we have been inundated with news reports confirming the sorry state of American education, telling us that European and Asian children outperform American students on standardized tests. That 63 percent of American students, ages eighteen to twenty-four, cannot find Iraq on a map; half cannot find the state of New York; and 11 percent cannot find the United States. That 28 percent of students in a different study think the American Revolution ended at the Battle of Gettysburg, and fewer than half recognized the words "We hold these truths to be self-evident, that all men are created equal . . ." as being from the Declaration of Independence. You know the studies I am talking about. The ones that say more people can name all five members of Homer Simpson's cartoon family than can name even five of the amendments to the Constitution that make up the Bill of Rights. Well, now those students are in Congress. And they are that much more incompetent than the previous generation of politicians. A third of them show up in Washington without ever having applied for a passport. (They quickly then get passports so they can enjoy the foreign boondoggles.) A greater knowledge of history, geography, and civics is demanded of third world immigrants applying for US citizenship than is possessed by your elected representatives.

And their grasp of finance and economics is no less abysmal. I once joined a group of financial people at a dinner for Iowa Republican Charles Grassley, then chairman of the Senate Finance Committee. Someone at the table expressed worry about the weak dollar to Grassley and asked what he was doing about it. Grassley answered that the dollar was neither the business of nor a matter of concern to his committee. Everyone at the table was stunned, not because he was prepared to do nothing about the dollar—which would be my advice anyway, let the market take its course—but because he showed so little knowledge of the financial markets. Not only was he wholly unaware of what was happening with the dollar, or what it meant, he was not aware of the fact that the value of the nation's currency might be of interest to his committee or that it fell within the boundaries of his responsibility. And he is one of the older members of the legislature; his passage through the American educational system predates that of many of his colleagues.

The people in Washington who have put the nation on life support make up a vast orchestra of incompetents, and the first among equals was the man who conducted that orchestra for nineteen years. He was not an elected but an appointed official: Federal Reserve chairman Alan Greenspan, the *Maestro* himself, so named by a benighted reporter, Bob Woodward, in an adoring book of the same title.

Greenspan, a mediocre Wall Street economist who was perpetually seeking government employment, had been flitting in and out of Washington for maybe fifteen years when President Reagan in 1987 finally rewarded him for his inadequacy. He served three subsequent presidents thereafter. A proponent of easy money, he printed it whenever things got tense, especially when things got tense for his former colleagues in New York. He did it in 1987 when the stock market crashed—a crash to which he contributed—and again in response to the Mexican peso crisis in 1994. He did it thrice more in the next few years. He was flooding the world with dollars in response to the Asia crisis when he started receiving hysterical calls from his friends at financial firms in New York, all of which were creditors of a Wall Street outfit called Long Term Capital Management, a hedge fund that was about to go belly-up.

Now, when the dental technician in Colorado Springs or the firefighter in Omaha puts in a call to the Fed, he or she is not going to get through. But when the CEO of Citibank calls, or the head of J.P. Morgan calls, the chairman himself gets on the line. And when the Fed chairman is told that this is the end of Western civilization as we know it, that this catastrophe could lead to the next Great Depression, the chairman, since he is not a very smart or very strong guy to begin with, starts bailing out everybody in sight. And that is just what Greenspan did for his friends, organizing rescues whenever financial types called.

If he had let some of those creditors go bankrupt, yes, there would have been difficulties. A bear market would almost certainly have followed. Earnings were already under pressure in the American economy. But if he had let the market take its course, Lehman Brothers would still be in business, and Bear Stearns would still be in business. Those firms would have taken such losses and suffered such pain that they would have fired a lot of incompetent people. Their balance sheets would have been impaired, but that would have been to their eventual benefit. It was all that excess money sloshing around on their books, available to now overconfident incompetents, that funded the highly questionable financial engineering that inevitably brought those companies down.

Greenspan refused to let the market work. He interfered with it in the boneheaded belief—along with a large dose of wishful thinking—that digging his friends out of trouble would be to everyone's benefit. He was a short-term thinker who operated out of panic. (Dr. Greenspan believed the Y2K changeover on January 1, 2000, would smite us all down, so he opened the printing presses until after the turn of the new millennium.) His greatest strengths were those of a politician. The way capitalism is supposed to work is that when people get in trouble, they fail. Smart, competent people come in, take over the assets, reorganize, and start again from a sound base. Greenspan's way was to prop up failure. He and the politicians were taking money from competent people, giving it to the incompetent people, and telling the incompetent people, "Here, the government is on your side. Now you can compete with the competent people with *their* money and our support." In the first place, it is horrid morality (not that politicians or bureaucrats have ever been driven by morality), and more, it is unsound economics. Recessions, bankruptcy, and financial failure are like forest fires. Forest fires are devastating, but they clean out the underbrush, they clear out the dead wood, and when they die, the forest grows back even stronger, from a healthier foundation.

"This process of Creative Destruction is the essential fact about capitalism. It is what capitalism consists in and what every capitalist concern has got to live in," wrote economist and political scientist Joseph Schumpeter in 1942.

Remember our old mobile phones, which created new fortunes only to be destroyed by the creativity of BlackBerrys, which in turn suffered destruction at the hands of Apple? Would you prefer to return to a world of land lines and constant searches for pay phones? Even Clark Kent has abandoned phone booths.

Had Greenspan allowed the market to work during his term, and especially in 1998 and 1999, we would have avoided the dot-com bubble. Firms on Wall Street would have had their metaphorical forest fires. When that bubble popped, he printed money again, which led to the housing bubble and the consumption bubble. He just could not print enough of the stuff. Blind to his own ineptitude, Greenspan sought and gained intellectual cover for his failed policies, bringing aboard an Ivy League academic, a tenured professor at Princeton with a PhD in economics, the yes-man who would succeed him at the Fed, Ben Bernanke.

In remarks before the National Economists Club in Washington after he joined the Fed's Board of Governors in 2002, Bernanke outlined his approach to monetary policy. "[T]he U.S.

government," he famously said, "has a technology, called a print-ing press (or today, its electronic equivalent), that allows it to pro-duce as many U.S. dollars as it wishes at essentially no cost. . . . We conclude that, under a paper-money system, a determined government can always generate higher spending and hence pos-itive inflation."

Call him Greenspan the Younger. Think of it as a dynasty. Together these two intellectual giants would initiate the great game of musical chairs that resulted in the global financial col-lapse of 2008.

While Greenspan was encouraging everyone to go out and spend money, to take an adjustable-rate mortgage and purchase a house—better yet, two or three houses—with no down payment, even if the buyer had no job; while he was holding down interest rates to promote the buying frenzy, on the absurd assumption that home prices could never go down; while the banks were pulling in astronomical fees making the bad loans, only to repackage and sell them as securities, thereby laying off risk with Greenspan's encouragement; while twenty-six-year-old kids at the rating agen-cies, kids just out of college with no experience in the markets, were cranking out hundreds of AAA ratings on the these junk derivatives every week; while all this was going on, I and people like me were saying that the emperor had no clothes.

I warned of the housing bubble as early as 2003 (see *Adven-ture Capitalist*), but as happens in all manias, skeptics are given very little credibility; they are either ridiculed or ignored. More than just predict the bubble, I put my money where my mouth was. Asked to justify my short sale of Citibank (at $50 a share) and Fannie Mae (at $60), asked how low I thought they could go, I was greeted with disbelief.

"I'll cover at five," I kept explaining to the press and to various analysts.

Both, of course, eventually went under a dollar.

So much for my trading calls.

In any game of musical chairs, as has happened in markets throughout history, the last guy in is the loser, the number of losers continues to grow, and everything spirals downward from there. Alan Greenspan, the master of the game, would have made things worse if he could, but his term at the Fed expired, and he left that part of the job to Bernanke. Along with guys like Hank Paulson.

HANK PAULSON WAS the secretary of the Treasury when, in 2008, after the subprime crisis hit, all the bankers in New York started ringing his phone off the hook, screaming that the world was coming to an end. Certainly, *their* world was coming to an end, or so it appeared. And of course when people like that are looking at the likelihood of going broke, what they do is call their friends in government. Paulson raced over to see President George W. Bush to tell him that the next Great Depression was upon us. Bush, who did not know anything in the first place, who could hardly spell "depression," told Paulson, "Do what you have to do," ceding responsibility for doing what was best for the country to the man who two years earlier had been the CEO of Goldman Sachs, one of the banks that was on hold back in Paulson's office. In eight years as chief executive officer, it was Paulson who had presided over the feeding frenzy in which a ravenous Goldman Sachs had gorged on subprime mortgages, the same junk paper that was now impossible to pawn off and on which his colleagues at the firm were presently choking.

At issue was not whether there was going to be a bailout check, but merely how big it was going to be. Whatever the number, Paulson could count on the concurrence of Bernanke, the know-nothing who was instrumental in creating the catastrophe, and that of Timothy Geithner, president of the New York Fed, the institution charged with supervising the banking system that had just gone south, and obviously a man who knew even less than Bernanke. The man who had fewer brains than either of them, George W. Bush, had been throwing the country's money down a rat hole for well on to eight years, at least $845 billion in Iraq alone over the course of the previous five (in direct costs to the US Treasury; an estimated $3 trillion in total costs). Another $700 billion in taxpayer bailout money meant absolutely nothing to him. He had already sailed the ship of state onto the rocks, and as the first man over the side, what better way to say good-bye to the people left aboard than to burn all the lifeboats behind him.

Paulson's defined-benefit pension plan at Goldman Sachs, intact in the wake of the eventual bailout, represented only a fraction of his net worth, which, when he departed the Treasury, was about $700 million. With no need for real work, he took a job in academia. Geithner, rewarded for his ineptitude, was named to replace him as Treasury secretary, pressed upon the incoming Obama administration by the New York banking community, which appreciated Geithner as the simple, little wimp sitting at the New York Fed who did whatever they asked. He was just the lackey they needed in Washington, the pushover who could be trusted to protect them when they told him the sky was falling. What did Obama know? He was probably as surprised as all of us when we came to find out that Geithner did not even know how to file his income tax. Bernanke, for his ineptitude, would be named to a second term as chairman of the Fed.

9

"CAPITALISM WITHOUT BANKRUPTCY IS
LIKE CHRISTIANITY WITHOUT HELL"

The Federal Reserve chairman, by law, is required to report twice a year to Congress on the Fed's monetary policy and is called to testify on numerous other issues at various times. I heard Bernanke testifying on one of these occasions—I was in a hotel room somewhere, and the television was on—and when asked to comment on the decline of the dollar, he answered that it was of absolutely no consequence except to Americans traveling abroad. I stopped what I was doing and looked very closely at the man on the TV screen, to see whether he was lying, or if he really did not know. Making a statement like that is a little bit like saying that whether the sun comes up in the east is of no consequence to the average American unless he or she happens to be looking east.

Say you own IBM, and it goes from $100 to $200. You have made money in US dollars, but if the value of the US dollar declines by 50 percent, you have not made any money at all—you cannot afford any more Scotch whiskey than you could before, you are no better-off in terms of your ability to buy a Toyota, both of which imports have effectively doubled in price. You are no better-off in terms of purchasing anything from abroad. Including things like petroleum. Even if the value of everything else stays the same, the fact that your dollar has declined means your standard of living has declined.

If the dollar goes down, imported tires go up in price, and that affects you as an American even if you do not buy your tires from Michelin, because Goodyear is going to raise its prices, if for no other reason than to cover the increased cost of imported rubber. If the dollar declines, Saudi Arabia, which sells oil denominated internationally in US dollars, is receiving less value. How long do you think that is going to be allowed to happen? For every sheik, the price of a Mercedes goes higher. Just to maintain their standard of living, the Saudis are going to have to raise the price of oil, and the smart and most effective way to do so is to cut the supply.

This is the nightmare of inflation. You may think you are better-off because your IBM shares have doubled in price—or maybe your salary has gone up—but then when you look around, you see that you are paying more for everything. You are paying more for gasoline. You are paying more for food. Your dollar is worth less and less against everything . . . against other currencies, against rice, against gold . . .

If the dollar goes down, the decline has a widespread effect on everything you as an American buy, everything you do, and pretty much everything that goes on in the rest of the world. It is Economics 101. Bernanke, testifying before Congress that the dollar's decline is inconsequential, did not look like he was lying, and one would have to assume that being under oath he would be a little bit constrained. So I came away with a realization that he knew even less than I thought.

Look back at the numerous pronouncements, the numerous projections Bernanke has made over the years, and it quickly becomes evident that he has seldom been right about anything. He knows little about economics or finance, he has no idea how markets work, and the only thing he truly understands about currency is how to print it. He has yet to figure out that the present crisis is one not of liquidity, but of solvency. There is plenty of liquidity around. Part of the reason for the crisis, in fact, is that American and European central banks, for ten or fifteen years, supplied too much liquidity to the market. There was too much cheap money available. It led to the housing and consumption bubbles, and when those bubbles burst, the world was left with a credit problem. Overextending themselves financially, people, institutions, and governments could not pay their obligations, an explosion of which resulted while the banks were taking all that garbage paper and turning it into subprime bonds. Loans today are not unavailable to people who are reasonably solvent; liquidity is not the problem. The problem is that too many people are bankrupt.

Bernanke does not seem to understand this. During the Great Depression, liquidity was indeed the problem. Thanks to misguided government policies, trade began to dry up, there was no liquidity to support the banks, and the whole system collapsed. Unable to distinguish between liquidity and solvency, Bernanke sees the current crisis as the 1930s all over again. It is the moment he has been waiting for all his life. His entire intellectual career has been devoted to the study of printing money. Give the guy a printing press, and he is going to run it as fast as he can, just as a guy with a hammer sees everything as a nail. But you do not solve the problem of too much debt with more debt. If printing money led to prosperity, Zimbabwe would be the most prosperous country in the world.

With Bernanke at the helm, nobody fails. Everybody gets a big bonus next year. Everybody keeps his Lamborghini, while our poor dental assistant in Colorado Springs is losing her job and her house because the government is pumping enormous amounts of money, collected from her and her fellow taxpayers, into the financial system to prop up bad assets at the banks. Rewarding failure, incompetence, and, in some cases, illegality, the government is buying bonds on what have already proved to be losing ventures run by mediocre people. It is throwing good money after bad, and thereby discouraging growth. All the competent people see all those bad assets sitting there, waiting to make a claim on the good, and are inevitably scared off, along with their money, leaving behind a stagnant economy with no new, dynamic forces at work.

In the early 1990s, Sweden, with a similar real estate bubble, faced its own collapse. But the government resisted bailing everyone out. A lot of people went bankrupt; it was a terrible two- or three-year period. But since then Sweden has boomed and is now one of the soundest economies in the world. Its currency today is much stronger than most, partly due to the country's suffering through that difficult period. The same thing happened in Mexico in 1994 and in Russia and Asia in the late 1990s. All these nations went through the wringer. People went bankrupt. And all emerged through the horrible pain thriving: sound, solid, and growing.

In the early 1990s, Japan experienced a big bubble in real estate and stocks. When I was traveling through the country by motorcycle on my first trip around the world, the price of a country club membership in Japan exceeded the price of a house. It was awe inspiring what people in Japan were willing to pay to play golf. The bubble was just peaking. The bubble eventually popped, and everything collapsed. And the government refused to let anyone fail. What resulted were what we now call "zombie" banks and "zombie" companies, institutions we identify as among "the walking dead." When I passed through Japan on my second trip around the world, ten years later, its suicide rate was higher than that of any developed country. Everyone was despondent, looking for security. Government jobs were highly sought after. The Japanese were referring to the 1990s as "the lost decade."

And now the lost decade has become two. Today, more than twenty years after the crash, the Japanese stock market is 75 percent below where it was in 1990. The suicide rate is still high, and the birthrate is among the lowest in the developed world. The sense of insecurity and lack of confidence going forward have not abated. Even in the depths of the Great Depression, the American stock market, dropping 90 percent, bottomed out only for a few months. In Japan, it has been over twenty years. In propping up the country's failing entities, the Japanese government extended the crisis. And this is the approach the United States has chosen to take.

America has had great collapses before. In 1907, the whole financial system went under. And yet in the twentieth century we came back strong. You can go back through American history and find examples of banks and insurance companies collapsing and states, counties, and municipalities going broke. After World War I, the United States had a serious economic setback, but the government balanced its budget while the Federal Reserve raised interest rates to curb inflation. We took our pain for several months but were then rewarded with the Roaring Twenties. Perhaps if people in Washington, D.C., read history or understood economics, we would stop using taxpayer money to prop up failure.

The world has suffered financial panics, financial disasters, since the beginning of time. It is not fun. It happens. And the world survives. Let us look at Japan again. In 1966, Japan experienced a staggering collapse. Every stockbroker in Japan went bankrupt. *Every* broker. Was it the end of the world? No. Every broker and every investment bank was *allowed* to go bankrupt. Over the next twenty-five years, Japan enjoyed phenomenal success, unexceeded by that of any nation in the second half of the twentieth century.

But the United States has chosen to follow in Japan's more recent footsteps. Politicians, worried about the next election, and pleading bankers, worried about the next bonus, carry the day. Like every entitled interest group in what is now the largest debtor nation in history, where everyone has his hand out and the federal government operates like Tammany Hall, the rich deserve payouts too. There will be no recession. There is no such thing as failure. There will be welfare for the rich. The Lamborghini and that house in the Hamptons are yours to keep—our firefighter in Omaha and a hardworking dental technician in Colorado Springs will happily see to that, even if they have to take second jobs to do so. Rather than force you to liquidate unsound assets, we will pay you to carry them on your books, or better yet, we will buy them. You will be compensated for your failure.

The Japanese talk of their two lost decades. We in America will have *at least* two, possibly more.

BEFORE THE SUBPRIME MELTDOWN, I was having lunch in Washington with Republican senator Richard Shelby, from my home state of Alabama, who at the time was chairman of the Senate Committee on Banking, Housing, and Urban Affairs, which supervises Fannie Mae. I said, "Dick, I hope this doesn't blow up on your watch," explaining that I was short Fannie Mae and that I believed the company was using phony bookkeeping and perpetrating a fraud. He thought about it for a minute, then said, "Well, you might be right," but he wanted me to understand that Fannie Mae and Freddie Mac made more political contributions to the people "in this town" than did any vested interest in the country. It was unlikely that the government would call them to account, much less that the guys cooking the books would go to prison, I was led to believe, for the simple reason that they were in everybody's pocket. Senator Shelby was and is a smart observer.

But while I know that examples of fraud can be found, I do not buy the fact that the crash was largely the result of criminal behavior. Much more widespread, and in the end even more infuriating, was the level of incompetence. I had far too many arguments back then, trying to convince others that it was a fraud—saying it was going to collapse, explaining why it was going to collapse—and having what appeared to be perfectly intelligent, ambitious, well-intentioned people telling me I was nuts. Everybody was taking the fast money, the easy money, and those who warned that it was not going to work were considered ridiculous. It was a wild time; there were staggering amounts of easy money around, thanks to the central bank, and just about anything you did would make you more of it, if you were fast enough and smart enough.

Few people realized that the house was built on sand. I do not think the people at Moody's who were putting out these AAA ratings really thought that some kind of evil conspiracy was at play. Most had their jobs on the line. People at the highest levels supported what they were doing. The chairman of the Fed, the secretary of the Treasury, everybody told them housing was safe. Greenspan urged Americans to take out loans, encouraged banks to create derivatives. He saw it as a way to get more money into the system; he convinced everybody it was good for the country. Fannie Mae said this stuff is sound. Wall Street really believed that the traders at Fannie Mae were smarter than everybody else. And the whole thing fed on itself. Alan Greenspan was getting his information from CNBC, which was getting it from some government bureaucracy, which was presumably getting it from him.

Chuck Prince, the head of Citibank, told the *Financial Times* in 2007, "As long as the music is playing, you've got to get up and dance. We're still dancing." I do not think Chuck Prince had a clue what the guys were doing down in his basement.

Yes, some people should have been sent to jail. It is difficult to see how Franklin Raines at Fannie Mae could not have known that what he was doing was crooked. He reported a rise in earnings of 15 percent every quarter, year after year. I know enough about the investment business to know that justifying those numbers is impossible. And yet Wall Street, making vast amounts of money selling the company's bonds, never questioned the claim. The people who did question it probably lost their jobs. If it were up to me, Raines would have been doing time in 2008, when instead, in defiance of all reason, his opinion was being solicited by the Obama campaign. If it were up to me, the guy running Merrill Lynch, Stan O'Neal, would have drawn a stretch at Leavenworth instead of the $160 million in severance he drew when Merrill threw him out the door of the company he helped to bring down.

It has been going on for thousands of years; history is replete with examples. The fact is people get greedy . . . bankers, clergymen, academics, politicians . . . especially when times are exceptionally good. People cut corners, do things they might not do under normal conditions, and because times are good, because there is so much prosperity, they are not held to account. Stocks go up. Investments pay off. The corners that are cut actually make people a lot of money. No one questions, or even cares, what happened—they are so happy with all the money they have made.

Manias cover a multitude of sins.

"You only find out who is swimming naked when the tide goes out," says Warren Buffett.

Following the Great Depression, Richard Whitney, president of the New York Stock Exchange, scion of the venerable family for which the Whitney Museum is named, was arrested and charged with embezzlement. He pleaded guilty and spent more than three years in Sing Sing. Had stocks continued to boom, nobody would have noticed or cared, because everybody would have made so much money. The same thing happened at Enron in 2001. Chief Financial Officer Andrew Fastow earned the praise of his colleagues for coming up with creative devices designed to hide the company's losses. He was a corporate hero until things started getting shaky on Wall Street, at which time the SEC discovered that he and his colleagues at Enron were defrauding the public (and that Fastow at the same time was defrauding his colleagues). He pleaded guilty to wire and securities fraud and, along with his coconspirators at the company, whom he immediately ratted out, he was shipped off to federal prison.

It happens not just in business. In the 1960s, in the America that I knew, it would have been inconceivable that one might accuse a Catholic priest of any kind of misbehavior. In doing so, one could expect to be ignored, if not actively held in contempt. But eventually, as the church became less powerful, people grew receptive to the idea that one might ask questions of the clergy and, furthermore, expect real answers. As the secular world intruded on the power of the priesthood, as times got tough and parishes dried up, only then did people come to identify the church hierarchy as an active sanctuary for criminal sex offenders; only then were they unafraid to say, "Yeah, these guys really are scumbags."

Misfeasance is not limited to business, nor is it anything new. It has been with us forever. And so too has incompetence. Neither should be rewarded. Economic slowdowns are inevitable. They have occurred regularly since the founding of the republic. We had one of the regular slowdowns in 2002. The one that began in 2007–2008 was much worse because the debt was up by a staggering amount. What will America do next time? We cannot quadruple our debt again. We cannot print reams of money again. Can we get away with it one more time? I doubt it. Certainly not two more times. Sometime in this decade the whole system is going to collapse. In 1907, when it collapsed, it could be saved because the United States was a rising nation. It was going from debtor to creditor status; it was on an ascending curve. It is now a debtor on a descending curve. In 2008, had the government allowed the losers to go broke, certain safety nets would have come into play—the government was then solvent enough. There would have been three horrible years, but by now we would have recovered. But that opportunity has passed. The next time it happens, there will not be enough money, and not nearly enough faith in government. Adam Smith said it takes a lot to bankrupt a country, but we are well along the path.

The Fed before 2008 had $800 billion on its books, mainly in government bonds. Since then that number has nearly quadrupled, and most of what appears on the balance sheet consists of garbage. Somebody has to pay for it. And who better than the American taxpayer? Bernanke says he will continue to buy bad assets. In doing so he is ensuring the demise of the central bank. If things get bad enough soon enough, we may abolish the Federal Reserve before it collapses. The United States has had three central banks in its history. The first two disappeared. This one will undoubtedly fail too.

Capital is agnostic. That is one of the truisms of the system under which we live. All capital cares about are security and getting the best return. Some raise this as a criticism, as evidence of the evils of capitalism. OK, fine, maybe it is. But it is also the way the world has worked for thousands of years. And nobody knows this better, or appreciates it more, than the capitalists who made fortunes riding the recent bull market over the edge. All should have been allowed to fail. The more of them that shared the fate of Lehman Brothers, the better-off the system would be.

As former astronaut Frank Borman, then CEO of Eastern Airlines, said, "Capitalism without bankruptcy is like Christianity without hell."

10

JOURNEY TO THE EAST

Happy was four when we moved to Asia, but we had started looking for a place to live when she was two. We spent the summer of
2005 in Shanghai, which, on paper, was our first choice, because
in my view it was going to be the world's next great city. Before
the Second World War, the Shanghai stock market was the largest in Asia, the largest exchange between London and New York.
The city had been a thriving, booming center of arts, culture, and
finance. The war ruined that, and Mao made it worse, but it was
clear to Paige and me, having spent time there on our Millennium
trip six years earlier, that Shanghai was now the place to be.

On my 1988 trip across China, I had visited the Shanghai
exchange, located at the end of an unpaved road in a rather ram-
shackle storefront. It occupied little more than a thousand square
feet of office space, overseen by a single attendant. To buy shares

you walked up to a counter and paid the attendant for your stock. An over-the-counter stock was exactly that. The attendant computed the transaction on an abacus. I bought a bank stock—only a few stocks were being publicly traded at the time—more for its historical than its intrinsic value. In the PBS documentary being filmed at the time, I predicted great things for China. "This is history being made," I said in the voice-over, as I purchased my shares. "Someday I am going to invest a lot of money in China. Before the revolution, China had the largest stock market in the Orient, and if I am right, someday it will again."

We took up residence in a serviced apartment in Shanghai, which is similar to living in a hotel. It is a setup designed for temporary but extended stays—a complete apartment, furnished, fitted out with cutlery, glasses, plates, linens, and such, and provided with housekeeping service—a living arrangement used extensively by corporations for employees on foreign assignment. You can just walk in, turn on the lights, plug in your computer, and you are home. And we loved everything about Shanghai, with one exception: the terrible air pollution. Before returning to New York, almost as an afterthought, we decided to spend three weeks in Singapore, taking similar accommodations there.

We did the same thing the following summer, in 2006, this time adding Hong Kong to the itinerary. The pollution in Hong Kong also was quite bad. By 2007, the trips had become our annual ritual. After visits to all three cities again—and spending time in Beijing and other Chinese cities, as well—we made the decision to move permanently to Singapore. While the air quality alone would have been enough to eliminate the Chinese cities from contention, there were other factors, as well. Singapore is essentially a Chinese city, 75 percent ethnically Chinese, but in Singapore, unlike Shanghai, English is an official language—*the* official language of government and business—and at the risk of overstating the case, I will remind you that, unlike my daughters, I am not a Mandarin-speaker. One of the factors weighing against our choosing Hong Kong, which like Shanghai is a very vibrant, exciting city, is that the Chinese spoken there is largely the Cantonese dialect, which is being replaced by Mandarin as the lingua franca of China.

So Singapore it was.

I remember, in April 2001, on our world tour, attending a Singapore Symphony Orchestra concert in the Botanic Gardens, and being struck by the absence of police. There was no law-enforcement presence of any kind. It occurred to me that a similar gathering in New York's Central Park would have brought out a small brigade, and I recall saying to Paige: "This would be a perfect place for children."

Adding to Singapore's appeal was the fact that the country's educational system is probably the best in the world, its health-care system is among the best, and—as is not the case everywhere in Asia—virtually everything in Singapore works, and works well. (Paige and I have an agreement that when we or the children require medical or dental care, we will board the next plane to Singapore from wherever we are in the world, because the quality of care one receives there is unsurpassed.) We applied for and received what is known as Permanent Resident (PR) status, which meant we could come and go as we pleased and allowed us to enroll the girls in public school.

Once on the ground in Singapore, we visited school after school and asked locals to recommend the one that was "most Chinese." We had expected to find a 100 percent Chinese curriculum, before learning that every primary school in Singapore is bilingual. The main medium of instruction is English, while everyone is also instructed in his or her mother tongue. The second language could be Tamil, Malay, or Mandarin, but everybody must learn in two languages until after the sixth grade. In Happy's school, Nanyang Primary, the mother tongue is Mandarin. One week is English week, in which all school announcements and all activities are in English. On the alternate weeks, they all are in Mandarin. The language of the classroom depends on the subject; for example, math is taught in English, civics in Mandarin. Baby Bee, who is four at the time of this writing, is enrolled in Nanyang Kindergarten. Only Mandarin is spoken in her classes; there is no English. In fact, the three teachers in her classroom, who are recent immigrants from China, are essentially monolingual. Of course, the beauty of being four years old is that, if you do not speak Mandarin, you pick it up in a matter of weeks, because that is what young children do.

Enrolling the children in Nanyang was not easy. Attendance there was much sought after, in large part due to its highly regarded principal, Madam Heng. It was the school to which the minister of education sent his children. Paige and I attended an open Primary 1 registration meeting, a presentation given by Madam Heng for interested parents, at which she explained the difficulties facing those seeking admission. We were the only Caucasians in the room—expatriates in Singapore tended to enroll their children in international private schools, where classes were conducted in their own languages—and we were full of ourselves, believing that Happy, our little blue-eyed blonde who spoke perfect Mandarin, would be snapped up immediately. If nothing else, cultural diversity and the school's need for geographical distribution, those attributes so helpful to my admission to Yale, would come into play.

Madam Heng impressed us with her intelligence, her commitment to discipline, and her incorporation of Chinese culture into the curriculum. When we took the opportunity to talk to her, she politely reminded us that there were numerous good schools in Singapore, and she advised us to look at all of them, her way of telling us not to get our hopes up. As she had said during her presentation, "In Singapore there are rules, and we play by the rules. As Singaporeans, you all know how it works." To us it was clear that Madam Heng, and Singaporeans in general, were not in the least interested in how it worked at Yale or Princeton. Among the rules we were glad to satisfy, leading to Happy's eventual admission, were that the family live nearby and that parents commit to doing regular volunteer work for the school. Paige learned about becoming a parent volunteer and went on to work with the English Department and the Reading Mums program. I gave presentations to members of the staff and helped with fund-raising. We moved from our apartment in the center of the city to within a kilometer of the school.

Chinese is a tonal language. I am not very good with tones, or with music, for that matter. The first time I took Paige dancing in Harlem, she asked, "Why don't you keep the beat?" I said, "I didn't know there was a beat, what beat?" She wound up leading when we danced, and whenever she would dance with somebody else, her instinct was to do the same—men would have to remind her to allow them to lead. There are four tones in Mandarin. You can say, "I would like to introduce you to my mother," but if you use the wrong tones when you say it, it might come out, "I would like to introduce you to my horse." Because I do not hear the tones, I usually stick to monotonous English. In some cases, where necessary, I can make myself understood in Mandarin. The first words I learned in China were the words for "cold beer."

Of course, in China, there are numerous regional dialects, and as a result not all Chinese people can talk to one another. They can write to one another, however, because the written language is the same for all of them. Sometimes you will see them trying to speak to one another in English while writing notes back and forth to one another in Chinese. They are not alone in the world; if you have ever seen a Bangladeshi speak to a Scotsman, for instance, you will notice that they both are speaking what they take for English, but with absolutely no comprehension of what one is saying to the other unless they write notes.

As Oscar Wilde said of England, "We have really everything in common with America nowadays except, of course, language."

In our house, when the children are home, two people, Paige and I, are speaking English, and two are speaking Mandarin, the housekeeper and the governess, who speak English to us but are allowed to speak only Mandarin to the children and to each other in the children's company. The girls' default language, as best I can determine, is English, at least when we are around, though at times they will start chattering away in Mandarin. I do not know why, or what sets it off. When they are teenagers, I am probably not going to understand what they are talking about even when they speak English, but I am *certainly* not going to know what the two of them are talking about when they speak Mandarin. They know that, and I am sure they will be saying all kinds of things behind Daddy's back. Which is fine.

For what it is worth, Baby Bee is taking Spanish lessons four hours a week. I do not know if it is going to take. I periodically run into a guy, an editor at Time Inc., who early in his career had been stationed in Paris. His five-year-old son, as a result, spoke flawless French. By the time the boy was eleven, however, and no longer living in France, he could speak no French at all. To this day, French might just as well be Greek to the young man.

Our first summer in Shanghai, when Happy was two, people would ask her, "How did you learn Chinese?" She could not comprehend the question, because she did not "learn" Chinese. Much the way I acquired English, she just grew up speaking Mandarin. All she knew was: *Some people speak like this and some people speak like that, and if I am going to speak with them, I speak the way they speak.* She did not know she had "learned" Chinese. With Baby Bee, you could almost see the lightbulb go off when her awareness of what was happening hit home: *Oh, I see what is going on: there are two different languages here. These are separate languages, I can speak them both, but not everyone can speak them both, including my poor, dumb daddy.* When she and I were together, she would whisper to Caucasians in English, and to Asians in Mandarin, "My daddy does not speak Chinese." I do not know if she was embarrassed and apologizing for her father's shameful ignorance, or if she was simply passing on information to others, politely filling them in so that they might understand what she herself now understood.

Happy and Baby Bee speak what is thought of as CCTV Mandarin, which is the received, standard Mandarin spoken on Chinese Central Television, the equivalent, if you will, of BBC English, considered the standard-bearer for received pronunciation of the Queen's English. Much of the Mandarin spoken by Singaporeans is quite poor. They travel to China and find that they are not easily understood. In 1979, Singapore launched its annual Speak Mandarin Campaign (SMC), an initiative to promote the use of Mandarin—good, standard Mandarin—and discourage the use of the various non-Mandarin Chinese dialects that pervade the society. The 2009 campaign included a series of videos featuring foreign children speaking fluent, correctly articulated Mandarin, among them various Caucasian children, including Happy and Baby Bee.

In New York, with our blessing and encouragement, Happy and her Chinese governess, Shirley, used to go to Chinatown to buy egg custards, a Chinese dessert. It was a good way for Shirley to expose Happy to Mandarin. Once, they were in a shop where only Mandarin was spoken, and Happy asked the shopkeeper for milk. The shopkeeper, in the way of a teacher, carried on a conversation with her in Mandarin.

"You drink milk?" she asked.   .

Happy replied, "Yes."

"What does your governess drink?"

"She drinks water."

"What does your father drink?"

"My father drinks watermelon juice."

"Happy, what does your mother drink?"

Happy answered in English.

"Wine," she said.

Shirley came home and told us the story, and, of course, Paige was mortified. Paige has a glass of wine with dinner now and then, but for the next week or two she drank anything but wine—"Oh, see, I'm drinking water"—lest the little girl think of her mother as some kind of drunk and spread the word around town.

THE JOY AND EXCITEMENT that Happy brought to our lives as our first child—watching her grow, helping her grow, simply spending time in her company—was more than I had ever known. Baby Bee was born five years later, in 2008, and our pleasure was doubled. We would probably have had a second child sooner, but with the onset of events in the fall of 2005, the thought of bringing another child into the world was beyond comprehension to me. In October of that year, just a few days short of my birthday, I had been accidentally dragged into someone else's criminal conspiracy. I would spend the next six years in the ugly no-man's-land of the American judicial system gaining vindication.

After creating the Rogers International Commodity Index in 1998, I eventually licensed it to such companies as UBS in

Switzerland and Daiwa Securities in Japan in exchange for a small fee. I maintained the index, and they created investment products based on it and offered them to their clients. In a separate setup, I had taken a majority share in a management company, Beeland Management, which offered two funds based on the index, the Rogers Raw Materials Fund and the Rogers International Raw Materials Fund. Leaving the day-to-day management of those funds to others, I set off around the world, hoping that I would be right about commodities.

By the time I returned home from the Millennium Adventure, it was already clear that the index I had created was a winner. It was outperforming all the other indexes handily. Clients of Beeland were all enjoying gains. But while investors were making money, Beeland Management was not. The company, run by a pair of managers in Chicago, was losing money, in part because the funds were so small. In the four years of its existence, while commodities were booming, the company, a small one that nobody, unfortunately, knew anything about, had raised only $20 million. A change was in order, and a few months after I returned, we brought in Walter Thomas Price of Uhlmann Price Securities, with headquarters in the Chicago Board of Trade, to run Beeland Management.

At the same time, I started appearing on television, talking up commodities, mentioning the funds and other funds based on the index. The funds started growing fairly rapidly. Within three years, benefiting from my return and, in larger part, from Tom Price's leadership—he did a brilliant job of saving things—the company had a few hundred million dollars under management.

Tom's chief responsibility was his own company. Beeland Management was almost something of a sideline. In the beginning, he had been able to handle things on his own. Now, due to the growth that Beeland had enjoyed under his guidance, he needed someone to oversee it full-time.

In 2005, I was invited to be the keynote speaker at the annual convention of the Futures Industry Association. While there, I had dinner with its chairman, Joseph Murphy, and some of his colleagues, who recommended a candidate that they agreed would be perfect to help with Tom's duties at Beeland. A few days later I received a telephone call from Murphy, who said he had since changed his mind. He knew of someone even better for the position, Robert Mercorella, an executive at the financial-services company Refco. The largest independent commodity broker in the world, and the largest broker on the Chicago Mercantile Exchange, Refco also happened to be the company that provided Murphy with his day job. Murphy at the time was head of Refco Global Futures. (I am sure I had heard of Refco, but the name did not sink in at the time. Refco had been the outfit that orchestrated Hillary Clinton's 1978 investment in cattle futures, turning her $1,000 into $100,000 within a mere ten months in what was a disguised payoff to Clinton.)

I met the CEO of Refco a couple of times, an Englishman named Phillip Bennett. He had gone to Cambridge University, I had gone to Oxford, so we babbled some about that. To my knowledge he was well respected in the industry. After all, he operated one of the industry's larger brokerage firms, with some two hundred thousand customers worldwide, and one of his officers, Murphy, was chairman of the Futures Industry Association, which is about as reputable as it gets. So Mercorella got the job. His mandate was to run Beeland full-time and raise the level of investment in the fund.

Tom Price had been using a respected, old-line brokerage, the Man Group, to execute trades. As soon as Mercorella arrived, he started talking about moving the fund from Man to Refco, which he said could offer a lot of improvements.

For example, there was not daily liquidity for the funds. You could redeem your shares only once a month. With Refco there would be daily liquidity. Also, certain companies, like Fidelity, would not let their customers buy the funds and keep them on deposit with their firms, for the simple reason that Uhlmann Price Securities was not well known to them; it was just not a big enough name in the industry then, though it is now. With a name like Refco behind the funds, that too would change. And another problem would be addressed. I had decided at the outset that I did not want the funds to have leverage; to borrow money would subject them to margin calls, which could turn out to be disastrous. A client would put up the full amount, and after meeting the margin requirement, the broker would take the balance and invest it in Treasury bills, paying the client the interest. It is fairly common and easy to do in commodities. The trade, however, in Treasuries was being handled inefficiently, and returns on the funds were inconsistent. Refco was in a position to manage the Treasury bills better and to execute the trades at lower commissions.

Moving the funds to Refco did offer several improvements,

and the move was under way when Murphy came to me in August and said, "Look, what we really want to do is buy your company." (It went a long way toward explaining the telephone call I had received from him after he and I had initially met, in which he recommended Mercorella, a Refco employee, for the position we were trying to fill, over the candidate he had originally endorsed.) The minority shareholders in Beeland Management had already agreed to a sweet deal for their share of the company. I entered negotiations with Refco for my majority share, but the deal fell through when Diapason Commodities Management in Switzerland, a company with which I had partnered to offer a similar fund in Europe, refused to sell. Refco saw no reason for two parallel funds.

So we went back to the original plan, and the movement of the funds from Man to Refco proceeded, a move intended to provide daily liquidity, broader distribution, and more credibility, to make the administration of the funds more efficient, more profitable, and more exciting for its investors.

They moved the money, $362 million, on Friday, October 7, 2005, from segregated accounts at Man, with clear, written instructions that it be deposited in similar accounts at Refco LLC. A segregated account is precisely as it is described. The money is held in the customer's name, and nobody can lay claim to it but the customer. It is like putting your money in a safe deposit box in a bank. If the bank goes broke, you remain unaffected; the money is still yours, and you can carry it out. What Refco did instead was deposit the funds at Refco Capital Markets, where the money was unprotected, where Refco management could access the customers' assets for its own purposes. This was a crime virtually unheard-of in the futures industry. Customer-segregated funds had not been violated in many decades.

It soon became clear that Refco was always grabbing customers' money, illegally shuffling it back and forth, even snatching it out of segregated accounts. Refco fooled a lot of people for a long time—while dealing with us, the company was in the process of going public, and the investment banks handling the IPO were Goldman Sachs, Bank of America, Credit Suisse, and First Boston, all of which had done extensive due diligence. If we had waited a single business day before moving the money, it would be somebody else's story to tell. But the timing was disastrous. By Monday, October 10, Refco was collapsing on news that Bennett had been perpetrating a massive fraud. He was arrested five days later, and on October 17, in what was reported as the fourth-largest bankruptcy filing in American history (a revised document was subsequently submitted), the now unprotected $362 million was frozen as part of Refco's assets.

Litigation lawyers started licking their chops, and the lawsuits started flying. They sued everyone in sight, including Beeland Management and me personally. I was sued in several courts, even though the company's offering documents stated clearly that I had nothing to do with the management of the company. None of us could figure out their case against us, since we too were victims of the Refco fraud. It just seemed a typical grab for a payoff by ambulance chasers—they offered to settle several times. We refused to pay them off because we knew our case was correct. Fortunately, the various courts and judges agreed with us, and the case never got close to a trial. Every suit was eventually tossed—the plaintiffs dropped out one by one, with the exception of a single investor in one of the funds, Clancy Ridley, who like his lawyer, Steve Clay, had been a classmate of mine at Yale. They held on to the very end, and then finally gave up, as the judge rejected every claim they made.

Beeland came out clean, I came out clean, and the shareholders deservedly got their money back plus a little more. (To get only a fraction of your money back in bankruptcies is usual.) But it all came at enormous personal cost. I was consumed by the whole thing for years, learning that even as an innocent bystander, I was going to be dragged through the courts forever, with attorneys trying to make it sound as though I had actually gone in with a gun in my hand and taken the money. It would continue until they abandoned their efforts, I assumed, not to win the legal case—that was never in the cards—but to make fighting it so disheartening and costly for me that I would pay them to go away. It was a devastating experience. In the beginning it was especially demoralizing. And by the end, I was completely worn out. I look at photos of me during these years and notice myself aging before my eyes. I had always heard of an event "aging" someone but had always thought it was just a figure of speech. Now I know better.

The time and energy that I was forced to devote to the fight made the thought of our having another child inconceivable. I was terribly depressed. Here I had pulled off this wonderful thing: I had developed this index, gotten the timing just right—one of the funds was growing rapidly—doing good things for the investors.

It was a great success, and then all of sudden these guys, supposedly vetted by everybody, were revealed to be nothing but crooks, and it was immediately clear that I was going to be sued.

I don't know that Paige ever knew how dispirited I felt. The anxiety made my hair go gray. It was all-devouring. Every morning I would turn on my computer to find a message from a lawyer—*Oh, my God, there's more*—knowing that whatever happened, even as we were winning, I was going to have to read another pile of documents and, if nothing else, respond. Every victory tasted less and less sweet. No individual triumph spelled the end of the battle. The hounding was constant. I tried not to let Paige know how depressed I was. I shielded her as much as I could. I grew up in an age where you did not talk about things like that so much. We had a two-year-old. I had to hold things together.

LITIGATION IS ONE of the healthiest growth industries in America. The United States has more lawyers than all other nations combined. The explosion of litigation accounts for a significant part of the expense of doing business in this country. The staggering cost of protecting oneself from lawsuits, double-checking, triple-checking everything, whether in business, education, or health care, is a driving force in decreasing the nation's competitiveness internationally.

We spend over 17 percent of our gross national product on health care now, which is more than twice the worldwide average and several points higher than that which is paid by the nation spending the second-greatest amount (Germany). And we have very little to show for it. You do not produce a superior liver operation if half of what you are doing is making sure you will not be sued. You certainly do not produce a *cheap* liver operation, running up all the extra expenses required—subjecting patients to unnecessary tests and procedures—to satisfy the requirements of your malpractice policy.

You do not produce competitive cars if your company is paying an exorbitant premium for health insurance, the price of which is driven by escalating medical costs—which are forced up by litigation. Doctors in Germany and Japan are not running up all these extra expenses. That means that German cars are more competitive than American cars; Japanese tractors are much more competitive than American tractors. Add to health-care-related expenses the cost to an American car company of liability insurance—the cost of shielding itself from all manner of lawsuits, including the most frivolous—and you can subtract that cost from what the manufacturer might otherwise spend on improving a car's performance. The money that General Motors puts into its cars to satisfy the financial needs of the nation's lawyers is money that BMW and Honda spend on engineering.

Allowing so litigious a culture to flourish reverberates through the US economy, affecting the cost of everything. Everybody who serves a hamburger has to factor into his operating expenses prodigious health-care and liability costs. And it is strictly an American phenomenon. This does not happen overseas. When we bought our homeowner's policy in Singapore, I asked the woman who sold it to us to please include litigation insurance. She told me it was available, but explained that it would hardly affect the policy's overall premium. "That doesn't happen here," she said. And she was right. But you could have said that in America, too, fifty years ago.

It is starting to happen in the United Kingdom, where large American law firms have branches, and also in Europe, but not nearly so much. The court systems in Europe are not nearly so tolerant of nuisance litigation as are courts in the United States. In most European courts, the rule is that the loser must pay the winner's legal expenses. It does not work that way in the United States, where filing a lawsuit costs you nothing. No matter how ridiculous your claim, you risk no financial loss.

Lawyers in liability suits work on a contingency basis, taking a percentage of what they win—or, more accurately, what you settle for. Seldom do they actually win. Nor, often, do they even try. They know that the defendant will come to realize that defending the suit will be far more expensive than settling it. In addition to costing you all your money even if you do win, an effectively targeted lawsuit can eat up all your time and energy and make your daily life miserable for years or, as Loews Corporation CEO Jimmy Tisch once said, a prison. In a variation on that famous adage concerning the markets: lawyers can remain irrational longer than you can remain solvent. Or sane.

You have seen these lawyers on television, advertising their services. They have employees whose job is to scour the news, watching for disasters, identifying victims, and more important, identifying people to sue. To raise the stakes, they venue-shop, choosing where to file a particular suit, trawling for jurisdictions and judges with histories of handing out higher awards. That was why I was sued in more than one court in two different states.

And I was lucky to have the cases thrown out while still in the preliminary stages, before massive depositions, for example. The threat of these is intended to put that much more pressure on defendants to settle: "Oh, no, they are going to depose my old third-grade teacher." Lawyers will rope in as many people as they can to amplify your mental anguish.

It was as a personal-injury attorney that former North Carolina senator John Edwards amassed the fortune that enabled him to run for public office. Indicted on multiple felony charges related to his 2008 presidential campaign, and facing up to thirty years in prison—a criminal, not a civil defendant—he found himself on the other side of the courtroom, in a fair approximation of hell, facing justice that is both rough and poetic, his prosecutors exploiting all the same mechanisms afforded by the system that enriched him, until the case ended in a mistrial. The judicial system does not take well to officers of the court who play fast and loose with the law, in those rare cases where it can be proved. In the criminal case against Refco, the government convicted Joseph P. Collins, the company's principal outside counsel, of securities fraud. The conviction was recently overturned on appeal, and it is unknown, at the time of this writing, whether the Justice Department will retry him.

The government did prevail against the perpetrators of the fraud. Bennett pleaded guilty to multiple charges and was sentenced to sixteen years in federal prison. His predecessor, Tone Grant, was tried and convicted and received ten years. Santo Maggio, CEO of Refco Securities, and Robert Trosten, Refco's former CFO, pleaded guilty to fraud and, both facing stiff sentences, offered to testify in exchange for leniency. (Trosten awaits sentencing. Maggio died in January 2012.) Joe Murphy was named an unindicted coconspirator.

Mercorella, if he had ever really left the company in the first place (some Refco insiders later told me he was planted as a double agent), went back to work at Refco, until it went under. In November, less than a month after the bankruptcy, Refco's futures and commodities business was sold to Man Financial, the brokerage division of the Man Group, until it was spun off as a separate public entity two years later and renamed MF Global. In October 2011, MF Global, whose CEO was former New Jersey governor Jon Corzine, made headlines when it filed the eighth-largest bankruptcy in US history after reporting a material shortfall in segregated customer funds estimated to be as much as $1.6 billion.

If at first you don't succeed . . .

11

NATIONS OF IMMIGRANTS

Housing in Singapore falls into three general categories: Housing and Development Board (HDB) flats; private apartments (including condominiums); and landed properties, which are privately owned residential units with individual ground contact. These last include attached houses, such as town houses, and what in Singapore are called "good class bungalows." A good class bungalow, which is what we rent, is a detached, single-family residence on its own property.

Only 12 percent of Singaporeans live in private housing. The vast majority, 88 percent, live in HDB flats. The government of Singapore, at its outset, realized that to build a stable society it needed to offer its citizens a stake in that society. To that end, it set out to provide housing for everybody. With Singapore's rapid economic development, today's HDB flats are far more elaborate than those built forty-five years ago. The earlier flats are slowly being torn down and replaced. The newer flats, many of them designed by internationally renowned architects, have the communal facilities we associate with high-end condominiums in the United States. Public housing is not a sign of diminished economic circumstances in Singapore. HDB flats cater to all income groups, although there are salary limits for first-time leases, and fully 95 percent of occupants now own their flats.

One of the keys to Singapore's success is its high savings and investment rate. It has the highest per capita savings rate in the world. Everybody saves and invests for the future, as is true in many Asian countries. In Singapore, however, saving is enforced. You are required to contribute 20 percent of your income to the Central Provident Fund (CPF), a national pension fund; it is matched by a 16 percent contribution made by your employer. (Contributions are made on wages up to a fixed monthly maximum; older workers and those earning below a fixed minimum, along with their employers, pay lower rates.) You can apply your savings to health care, to education, or to buying a home. It is your own money in your own separate account, but spending your CPF savings on a Maserati, nights at the disco, or a vacation in Cancún cannot happen here.

We live only about a half a mile from the school, and I am known by some people in Singapore as the white guy who takes his kids to school on a bicycle. The bike, actually a trike, with three wheels, is a modern Dutch contraption, a Taga, with a wooden carriage in front that seats two. Singapore, like California, is a car society. Fifty years ago, Singaporeans all rode bicycles, but as they got rich, one of the first things they did, in signaling their prosperity, was get rid of the bicycles and purchase automobiles. The same thing happened in Shanghai and other Asian cities. But traffic is a growing problem now, and bicycles are making a comeback.

To cut down on traffic congestion during peak hours on various roads, Singapore in 1998 instituted the Electronic Road Pricing (ERP) system, an automated toll-collecting mechanism. Sensors located on overhead gantries communicate with an In-Vehicle Unit (IU) attached to your car. The IU holds a cash card from which payment for road use is automatically deducted. You can do many things with your ERP account that make life very simple. You go into a parking lot, for example, and the fee is clocked automatically. In the United States, we pay toll collectors and parking lot attendants. Not in Singapore. It is a small island, and cluttering it up with tollbooths would make things even worse.

Of all the things Singapore has gotten right, one of the more important is education. My chief reason for coming here was to broaden my children's education. I wanted them to know Asia, I wanted them to know Mandarin, but I also knew that in Singapore the formal schooling they received would be rigorous. When I was in secondary school in the 1950s, students who were serious about tests and homework were as often as not ridiculed for their work ethic. Even at Yale, some students who studied hard were known for that reason as "weenies." I cannot say whether things since then have changed dramatically in the United States. I know that in Singapore there is no such thing as a weenie. Here the importance of education is an understanding that permeates the whole culture.

Happy came home one day and announced that at the American School, a big international school here, students do not have homework in the second grade. She was not angry. She was making a matter-of-fact report: here she was, given at least two hours of homework a day beginning in first grade, and at the American School they were given none. I have to admit that sometimes I wonder if I am actually right to encourage her to spend so much time on her schoolwork. Should she be worrying so much about the work she brings home? Would she be better-off at her age just playing? I find myself asking, Will the amount of work these kids do at age eight eventually burn them out? What is going to happen when Happy is eighteen? She might just say, hell, I want to join the army so I do not have to do all this schoolwork again. She is good, she thrives on it, yet no matter how well or poorly she does, I question whether it is going to affect her when she is forty-two. Supposing there is the chance that it might, and being an immigrant family, if not a typical one, we tend to follow the lead of our fellow Singaporeans.

I had a conversation recently with a very dynamic, successful CEO in China, a mother in her forties, a PhD. She has a son, and I was telling her about my daughters. She told me I was making a mistake with Happy. Schoolgirls should just play, she said, they should have fun. This was a woman who was born in the 1970s. She had somehow worked her way through to a PhD at a time when China was going through dramatic changes. And she was telling me to forget about school, to take it easy—if Happy wants to get a PhD, she said, fine, she will do it, but there is no reason to push her. Let her go, leave her alone, the woman told me. And I have to tell you that what she said resonated. Kids today seem to be terribly overscheduled. I remember my childhood—the door was always open and we went outside. So I wonder if I am doing the right thing with the girls.

On standardized international tests, Singapore always comes out near the top. Asian children, in general, always come out ahead of American children on such tests. In the United States, children are taught self-esteem. Paige and I are of the opinion that you earn self-esteem. Happy in her first two years finished in the top five of her class. This year, so far, she is near the top in Chinese. So Happy has earned her self-esteem. You really have to work here to do well in school, and it seems to carry over into real life. I believe it is one reason Asians are doing so well in the world. America is not competitive, and you can trace it back to attitudes in homes and in schools.

In Singapore, there is an educational ordeal called the Public School Leaving Examination (PSLE). Everybody in the sixth grade takes it, and how you perform on it pretty well determines your future, at least for a while. A twelve-year-old who scores at the top on this nationwide test gets his or her photograph—and that of his or her parents—displayed on the front page of the newspaper here when the results are announced. It is but one example of the emphasis placed on education in this part of the world. In the press, numerous column inches are dedicated to stories of kids who are doing well in school. It is the kind of attention reserved for high school and college athletes in the United States.

There is one tradition associated with Happy's American education that we did import from home when we took up residence in Singapore—no television. In the forty years that I lived in New York, I did not have a TV. I can think of no good reason to own one now. How influential my viewpoint will prove to be is open to question. When we travel, the first thing Happy does after we check in to a hotel is turn on the television. And she wants to sit there and watch it all day.

"OK, Happy, let's go."

"I don't want to go out, I want to watch TV."

"Happy, it's in German."

"I don't care. I'll learn German."

We all love Vienna, and when there we sometimes stay at the fancy Hotel Sacher, a five-star hotel famous for, among other things, its specialty of the house, the Sachertorte, a chocolate delicacy invented in 1832 by the father of the hotel's founder. Opened in 1876, the hotel served as British headquarters during the four-power occupation of Vienna after the Second World War. Happy once told us that when she is twenty, she is going to move away from home, get an apartment in the Sacher Hotel, and watch television all day, and that there is nothing we can do about it.

Baby Bee has not gotten to that point yet, but I suspect the day is coming.

Life has been good to us in Singapore, and I see no reason to leave. Of course, I saw no reason to leave New York, where I had been living for forty years. If there is a reason to leave, then I presume—I hope—I will be smart enough to leave. The Chinese have an expression, rags to rags in three generations. I think every culture has a variation on the same expression. We have it in America too. Rags to riches then back to rags. A member of the family strikes it rich, and the person's grandchildren, maybe the great-grandchildren, wind up back on the dole. The Chinese have had the expression for centuries. It applies to countries as well as families. Countries rise, and then they decline. It happened to the British and to the Spanish; it happened to Egypt and Rome; it is happening to the United States.

China is alone in having had three or four periods of greatness (followed by long periods of great decline). Conceivably, it has something to do with philosophy. Throughout Chinese history one sees great cultural emphasis placed on education. Confucianism holds teachers and scholars in high esteem. Even today in China you can occasionally still see plaques, erected under the emperors, going back hundreds of years, commemorating the scholar-bureaucrats who excelled on the imperial civil service examinations.

But Singapore is staggeringly successful. It has so much accumulated wealth and expertise that I cannot see it losing them in my lifetime unless some serious mistakes are made. Baby Bee's lifetime? Well, that is a long time. That is a hundred years from now.

Singapore is a nation of immigrants. Fifty years ago it consisted of a million people living in a swamp. The population is now five million. Immigrants started coming when the British were running the place. Today, almost a quarter of Singaporean citizens and permanent residents and nearly half of the overall population were born outside the country. Singapore has encouraged immigration for a couple of reasons. In the beginning, the country needed the capital and the expertise. Today the country promotes immigration because it is facing a serious demographic problem. The population is aging rapidly. The country's fertility rate is among the lowest in the world.

The demographic situation in Singapore is so dire that the government has overseen the construction of new flats—one-and-a-half flats—one standard apartment, and adjacent to it a studio apartment, where one can house an aging parent. The government has offered incentives to encourage couples to have babies. It has set up dating agencies to increase the number of couples. But it continues to rely heavily on immigration. Being as small as it is, the country can be selective, seeking smart, successful, educated immigrants, even while being mindful that it needs people to drive the buses. Other countries—the United States, for example, with 300 million people—do not enjoy a similar luxury.

Unfortunately, in the last couple of years, Singapore has experienced a bit of a backlash. Residents complain that the buses are too crowded, that the schools are too crowded, none of which is true, but the government's response has been to slow immigration fairly dramatically. Giving people time to accommodate to the influx of outsiders, the government, at least in the near term, is acting out of political expediency. In the 2011 election, the People's Action Party (PAP), which has won every election since the advent of self-government, lost six of the eighty-seven elected seats in parliament to the Workers' Party. It was the opposition's best result since independence.

Singapore, in one way, is no different from any other country in the world: for any number of ailments, outsiders make for convenient scapegoats. When people are looking for people to blame, they blame the foreigners first. Their language is different, their religion is different, their skin is different, their food is different, their food smells bad—*they* smell bad . . . I have heard these things said about foreigners all over the world, especially when things are not going well. In Singapore it falls on the Malays, Indians, Eurasians, even the Chinese. *They are not like my grandparents who came here from China.* In fact, they may be superior to your grandparents, having been selected for their skills and educational qualifications.

Nowhere is intolerance making more headlines today than in the state where I grew up. In June 2011, the state of Alabama, in a fit of xenophobia, passed a bill called HB 56, considered to be the most draconian anti-immigration law in the country. And its impact on the state has been catastrophic. In September of that year, when the law went into effect, thousands of immigrants fled the state in fear, abandoning jobs, schools, and homes. Crops were left to rot in the fields, breaking the back of the state's $5.5 billion agricultural industry. Reconstruction of buildings destroyed by the devastating tornadoes of the previous April slowed to a standstill as 25 percent of Alabama's construction workers left the state.

Counter to claims made by its political sponsors that the bill was engineered to free up jobs for unemployed Americans, Alabamans have proved unwilling to fill the jobs that have been vacated by the workers they vilify. There has been no growth in the job sectors where Hispanics typically work. It is estimated that up to 140,000 jobs in the state could be lost. If you factor in the savings to the state in health care and social services that the bill's supporters achieved, the overall loss to the state is estimated to be about $11 billion, or 6 percent of GDP, which does not include losses of $339 million in state and local tax revenue.

In November 2011, shortly after the bill went into force, a Mercedes-Benz executive from Germany, on business at the company's plant outside Tuscaloosa, was arrested and jailed by local police on suspicion of being an illegal alien when he was unable to produce his passport, which he had left at his hotel. The director of the state's Department of Homeland Security—yes, Alabama has one—said, "It sounds like the officer followed the statute correctly." A month later a Japanese manager assigned to the Honda Motors plant in Lincoln was stopped by police and cited for violating the statute by not being in possession of a valid driver's license (issued either by Alabama or by his native Japan—his international license, supported by his passport, was insufficient).

Foreign companies employ 5 percent of Alabama's population. The Spanish owner of BBVA Compass has already canceled a proposed $80 million bank tower in Birmingham, and China's Golden Dragon Precise Copper Tube Group is reconsidering plans to build a $100 million plant in Thomasville. Immigration advocates are pressuring Korean automaker Hyundai, whose $1.4 billion plant in Montgomery accounts for 2 percent of Alabama's GDP, to take a stand against the law.

The catastrophic economic impact of the bill makes Alabama legislators look foolish. The social and humanitarian costs of xenophobia speak for themselves. The constitutionality of the law is being challenged in the federal courts. One judge described the legislative debate that led to the law as "laced with derogatory comments about Hispanics." The White House opposes the law, asserting that jurisdiction over immigration is reserved to the federal government.

In whatever way the federal question is resolved, the state legislators who drafted the law, drenched in the economic and political blowback of their own stupidity, have been forced to revisit the bill. Where the dice will fall is anyone's guess.

The immigration battle continues in various states in various ways.

AMERICA'S GREATEST PROSPERITY came before immigration laws were instituted. They were spawned in the 1920s, out of fear and monumental ignorance, at the instigation of the Ku Klux Klan, with a prejudice against all immigrants: Italians, Catholics, Jews, anyone remotely different. Before that our borders were open. As were borders all over the world. Marco Polo did not have a passport. Nor did Christopher Columbus. Had our forebears needed permission to come to the United States, America never would have been what it became. We might not have had an America if the Marquis de Lafayette or Thomas Paine had been required to obtain visas. Some of the prominent American industrialists who made us great were immigrants, including Andrew Carnegie and John Jacob Astor.

Throughout history the most prosperous societies have been those that were open to the world. In the late fourteenth century, if people wanted to pack up and move to Samarkand, that is what they did. A preeminent city on the Silk Road between China and the Mediterranean, Samarkand was a rich and wildly thriving cultural crossroads. It was the capital of Tamerlane's Mongol empire, a great international hodgepodge, a melting pot of languages and religions. Four hundred years earlier, at the turn of the first millennium A.D., the most populous city in the world was Córdoba, in Andalusian Spain, the capital of an Islamic caliphate that flourished for a hundred years. Ethnically, culturally, and religiously diverse, the city was an intellectual center supporting one of the largest libraries in the world, and it gave rise to significant advances in science, philosophy, geography, history, and the arts.

People flocked to cities like these from all over the world, and the cities became even greater. It is what happens when you leave your doors open. Deng Xiaoping said that if you open a window some flies will come in, but doing so is part of admitting sunshine and fresh air.

In Sydney, Australia, when Paige and I were circling the world, one of our dinner companions, a corporate executive, was complaining about immigrants. I found this somewhat pretentious, given that the businessman in question and his wife were immigrants themselves. They were New Zealanders. When I reminded him of this, the best he could come up with, a response that made perfect sense to him, was: "We were different. It was different then." You run into this kind of thinking all the time: *Close the door now that I am inside.* I got the same response on a speaking tour in California from an American businessman whose family had immigrated to the United States from Europe when he was a young adult. "My family was different," he said. The most vehement anti-immigration sentiment sometimes comes from immigrants themselves.

If it were up to me, borders to all countries would be open. It would promote a more natural ebb and flow, make every country more dynamic. New blood, new capital, new ideas. These always benefit a society and an economy. They make us more creative. Throughout history, the people most eager to immigrate have been those people who are ambitious, smart, and energetic, the kind of people you would want to hire. It is no different today than it was in Tamerlane's time.

I cannot remember where I was when I saw it, but I remember once seeing a news report about a Cuban who had strapped himself to a barrel, put to sea, and navigated the Straits of Florida, crossing to the United States. Well, the police were there on the beach when he arrived, waiting to arrest him and deport him back to Cuba. If I had been there when he came ashore, I would have hired him on the spot. Rather than arrest the guy, I would have given him a job. He is just the kind of person I would want working for me, someone brave enough and driven enough to do that, and smart enough to figure out how to do it and survive. You want people like that in your employ, and you want people like that living in America. They are the kinds of people who come to a new country and build companies and create fortunes.

I remember, in 1990, when I rode my motorcycle around the world, arriving in Siberia, in the port city of Nakhodka, about fifty miles east of Vladivostok. A port official asked me how it was that I was allowed to travel—not travel to Russia, but travel *from* the United States: Can you just leave whenever you wish and go back whenever you wish? he wanted to know. Among the lies he had been told living under Soviet communism was that throughout the world people were not allowed to leave their own countries, and if they did, they were not allowed to go back. He seemed unsurprised when I answered yes. He probably had received similar replies from the various foreign sailors whose ships were anchored in Nakhodka Bay. But his question illustrates my point. Immigrants and visitors offer exposure to the outside world, which in the end can only be good.

"Is it not delightful," Confucius wrote, "to have friends come from distant quarters?"

That was twenty-five hundred years ago. Today, to have friends come from distant quarters is not merely delightful but absolutely necessary for countries whose populations are aging. Singapore is not alone in that regard. Europe is aging rapidly. We are even seeing a graying of America. It is a problem in much of the developed world, and one to which societies know they have to adjust. Retirees do not build factories, start businesses, and hire people. They are not those members of society who generate capital, nor do we expect them to be. Drawing on the social services to which they are entitled, aging citizens are consumers, not producers, of capital. It is young people of working age who produce it.

Birthrates in the developed world have declined with an increase in prosperity. People with money do not need children to support them in their old age, or to care for them in old age. Nor, in a modern industrial society, do people need children to work on the farm. It costs a lot of money to raise children. Why spend it sending a second or third kid to private school in Manhattan when you can spend it on a trip to the Bahamas? Even in the absence of a large nest egg, people can fall back today on a social safety net that did not exist, say, a century ago. Nor is religion as strong a force as it once was. Catholics, with the encouragement of the Church, have always been known for having lots of children. Today, two predominantly Catholic countries, Italy and Spain, have among the lowest birthrates in the world.

In the absence of immigration, there is only one way for a nation to address its need for young people, and that is to give birth to more babies. I suppose there is a second way—in a demographic repurposing of Jonathan Swift's *A Modest Proposal*, you could sell the old folks as food. But no one is suggesting Plan B. Japan is the laboratory case. Japan's birthrate is one of the lowest and its life expectancy one of the highest in the world. There are more pets in Japan than there are children. The country is on its way to being nothing but an old age home, with lots of old people and no one to support them. The Japanese government estimates that in fifty years, 40 percent of the country's population will be sixty-five or older. What makes the problem that much more difficult to solve is Japan's notorious insularity. Japan is one of the more xenophobic countries on earth. Racism there, the United Nations reported in 2005, is "deep and profound." The country is no more eager to boost immigration than it is to go to Plan B.

Any discourse on the free flow of people necessarily leads to a consideration of freedom itself, and amid the transitions taking place in the world, few things are in more significant flux than the freedom we take for granted—or used to—in the United States.

··

12

LAND OF THE FREE?

*The power of the Executive to cast a man into prison without
formulating any charge known to the law, and particularly to
deny him the judgment of his peers, is in the highest degree
odious and is the foundation of all totalitarian government
whether Nazi or Communist.*

—WINSTON CHURCHILL

President George W. Bush, in explaining to the nation why members of al-Qaeda attacked the United States on September 11,
2001, told us, "They hate our freedoms. . . ." Let us ignore, for
the sake of argument, the sheer idiocy of his analysis, and consider his response to the terrorists. He accommodated them. In
the context of his own argument, his decision was to give them
what they wanted. Within six weeks of the attack, Bush signed
legislation that deprived American citizens of liberties that they
had enjoyed for more than two hundred years, the very freedoms,
according to him, that the terrorists hated.

The Patriot Act, the legislation Bush pushed for and signed
into law, and within the constraints of which we Americans now
live, includes the kinds of provisions with which the jihadis of
al-Qaeda are eminently familiar. It incorporates the kinds of

statutes that hold sway in the countries where they live, authoritarian states, where denial of rights by the government helps produce terrorists like them. Now we, too, live in a nation of warrantless wiretaps, unreasonable searches and seizure, indefinite detention, and institutionalized torture. Just like them. Now we, too, have a domestic surveillance apparatus, the ominously titled Department of Homeland Security.

Having a problem with one of your neighbors? You do not like the smell of his food? Drop a dime on him, call Homeland Security, say that the guy has been acting strange. The government will dump him in Gitmo for five or six years, throw him some questions, get him out of your hair for a while. An American citizen? Nobody cares. In Yemen, in September 2011, the CIA dropped a drone on two American citizens. Guilty? Perhaps. One will never know. No arrest, no lawyer, no judge or jury, no trial . . . There is a secret committee that handles these things now. It is a new day in the land of the free.

Certainly, in America, in the course of our history, we have had our share of lynch mobs, innocent people being persecuted by the state and the mob. But at least in theory, if not always in fact, safeguards against such persecution existed. At least in theory, the government was prohibited from executing even guilty people without trial. What has changed is not that the government has overstepped its authority—Abraham Lincoln went as far as to suspend habeas corpus—but that the government's doing so has become acceptable, celebrated in some cases.

I have learned to distrust the government—I recommend that every American do so—and my skepticism has been evident for at least forty-five years. While attending Officers Candidate School at Fort Lee, Virginia, in 1967, I joined one hundred thousand or so war protesters in that year's famous march on the Pentagon. I fear, however, that my skepticism is merely generational. My father's generation, or so it seemed to me, believed everything it was told. And the generation that is coming of age today is reminiscent of my father's much more than it is of mine. Not that Americans today believe everything the government says, but that they somehow feel no need to believe it. From the body counts of Vietnam to the equally fictitious justifications for invading Iraq, little has changed except the public's willingness to swallow government distortions and spin. Truth is the first casualty of war, it is said, and while that proposition has always been descriptive, it has now become weirdly prescriptive: the US political establishment has taken it to mean that war grants the government the *license* to lie. And what better way for elected officials to run the country than by keeping the nation perpetually at war, as it has since 2001.

The United States was founded on a principle that was decidedly foreign to the rest of the world in the late eighteenth century: that your rights are not something the government gives you, but something the government cannot take away. It was a revolutionary notion, and it took a revolution to make it real. Well, we are not that country anymore. We are now a country where the primacy of the individual is subordinated to the prerogatives of the state.

In 1980, we elected a president who paid lip service, if nothing else, to the majority's desire to "get government off the backs of the people." In 2004 we reelected a president whose popularity derived from his implied promise to keep the people off the government's back. We are now finally structuring a government like the ones that immigrants and refugees for two hundred years have been coming here to escape. We have outgrown our founding fathers. We are now the sons and daughters that one of them, in 1759, warned against our becoming.

"Those who would give up essential liberty to purchase a little temporary safety," said Benjamin Franklin, "deserve neither liberty nor safety."

Content to give up our claim to being the land of the free, we as a nation, by lying down and ceding our rights to a government that induces us to be frightened, will find it somewhat problematic to describe ourselves as the home of the brave.

BY THE TIME this book is published, a law will have taken effect that makes it effectively impossible for Americans to open bank accounts outside the country. Say you are an executive at Ford, and you are transferred to its German subsidiary. You open a local bank account to pay your bills and to withdraw euros. Under the Foreign Account Tax Compliance Act (FATCA), scheduled to take effect January 1, 2013, it may prove too onerous for that foreign bank to keep you as a customer.

It has long been a requirement that Americans report all their foreign bank accounts to the US government, as I do when paying my taxes. But already the officers of two foreign banks where I have had accounts for years—the existence of which I have routinely reported, as required by law—have called to say, sorry, we love you, but we do not take Americans anymore, and we are getting rid of the ones we have. Why? Because the disclosure requirements that have always been my responsibility are now being imposed upon them, and in even more burdensome form.

Under the new law, foreign institutions that do not sign an agreement with the IRS to police US customer accounts face a punitive 30 percent withholding on their American-derived proceeds. These institutions do not consider themselves branches of the US Treasury Department; they are not being paid to do all the extra work necessary to identify and file reports on their customers—imposing taxes on certain customer deposits; and finding the exorbitant costs of such compliance prohibitive, they are just closing out American citizens. There is always the added risk of suits and fines, even if there is a mistake, so the efficient solution is to bar Americans. European banks like Deutsche Bank, Credit Suisse, and HSBC started closing all US brokerage accounts in 2011.

The fear of capital flight as a result of the law appears to be justified. I am told that in London there is a six-month waiting list to give up your American citizenship, in Geneva a fourteen-month wait. The number of people who did this fifty years ago, even thirty years ago, was minuscule. Probably the most famous example is John Templeton, the billionaire mutual fund pioneer and philanthropist who renounced his American citizenship in 1964 to avoid paying more than $100 million in taxes on the sale of his international investment fund, Templeton Growth. He took up residence in the Bahamas and became a naturalized citizen there and in the United Kingdom.

Today, for such renunciation, there are waiting lists. At the US Consulate in Singapore, there is a price list on the wall, itemizing the charges for various services, and both this year's and last year's prices are posted. Recently I was at the consulate to renew a passport, and I noticed that the charge for renouncing your citizenship today is $450. In 2010, it was free (up until July of that year). And there was a time, apparently, when you could just walk in and do it without an appointment. Now, of course, you need one. You have to go through a procedure in which a consular officer has an opportunity to talk you out of it, sending you away, telling you to come back, using delaying tactics and whatever else it takes to dissuade you, in part to protect you—to make sure that your renunciation is voluntary and intentional—and in part because renouncing your citizenship these days has become something of a movement.

The inability of Americans to keep foreign accounts is only one reason behind the trend. Banking regulations under the Patriot Act are making it increasingly harder for Americans living abroad to keep accounts in US-based banks. According to American Citizens Abroad, an advocacy group based in Geneva, the US banks, cowed by the antiterrorist provisions of the act, are closing the accounts of longtime customers with addresses outside the United States "as acts of prudent self-defense," the result being that expatriates have now become "toxic citizens."

The United States is one of the few countries in the world that impose taxes based on citizenship rather than residency. American expatriates are subject to double taxation. They pay US taxes on top of the taxes they pay to the countries in which they reside.

If you give up your US citizenship and you have a net worth of over $2 million, there is an assumption that you are doing it for tax reasons. Your wish may be to become a Buddhist monk and live penniless in the hills of Tibet. But if your net worth, marked-to-market, exceeds the aforementioned $2 million (or your average net tax liability for the previous five years surpasses a certain threshold), the government says you are headed to Shangri-La, not to meditate, but to avoid taxes. And therefore you have to pay an expatriation tax, an exit tax calculated on the value of your assets. *The Economist* called it America's Berlin Wall. The United States has joined the former East Germany, North Korea, Cuba, Iran, the former USSR, and 1930s Germany on the list of countries with laws engineered to keep citizens in, and in some cases prevent their return should those citizens manage to leave.

SO FAR, under FATCA there is a $50,000 threshold. On US customer accounts under that amount, foreign banks need not report. Normal checking and savings accounts in most countries have yet to be affected. But it is probable that very soon I will be unable to maintain a bank account locally to pay my electricity bill. Unless, of course . . . Yes, Citibank has a branch in Singapore. I do not have an account there, but it may be that if no other bank will take me, then I and all the other Americans in Singapore will have no choice but to transfer our accounts there, or to one of the other American banks (Chase and Bank of America) that also have branches here.

If members of Congress had that in mind when they wrote the new law, as some European bankers believe, the law can be seen as a form of protectionism. It can be viewed as a restraint of trade. And it would not be naive for foreign bankers to assume that Citibank probably helped write it. Citibank does have an extensive offshore network, and Congress does have a way of protecting its friends.

In 2005, the US House of Representatives prevented the Chinese National Offshore Oil Corporation (CNOOC) from acquiring Union Oil of California. Unocal is now a wholly owned subsidiary of Chevron, America's fourth-largest corporation. In 2006, under pressure from Congress, Dubai Ports World was forced to sell its newly acquired terminal operations at American ports to a division of US insurance giant AIG—despite Dubai's being one of our staunchest allies (part of the US fleet is berthed there). Politicians hollered national security, but restraint of trade on behalf of their constituents was what motivated each of those efforts.

We did it to the Chinese, we did it to our great ally the United Arab Emirates, and soon thereafter other countries, like France and Brazil, were following our lead, taking cover from our willingness to engage in protectionist measures. When Brazil put tariffs on cars imported from China, it cited Congress's continuing threats to slap tariffs on the Chinese, as US representatives beat their breasts over China's currency manipulation. The prevailing international sentiment is that if America can do it, so can we. The world is flirting with the "beggar thy neighbor" policies that deepened the Great Depression.

The stock market crash of 1929 brought down some rich people, mostly the investors attracted by the bubble that preceded it, but Americans directly affected by the popping of the bubble were few in number. It was not the crash itself, as dramatic as it was, that made the Depression "Great." Certainly, the coming economic setback would have been somewhat worse than normal—in those days banks could buy stocks, and a lot of small banks around the country got in trouble as a result of the mania—but then along came the politicians. The Smoot-Hawley Tariff enacted in 1930 and the subsequent retaliatory tariffs leveled by US trading partners turned what would have been a worse-than-normal recession into the Great Depression.

We do not have an outright trade war yet, but we are taking small steps in that direction. The rising tide of protectionism can be seen in restrictions on the free flow of capital. Call it "beggar thy neighbor's currency." Seeking security and high return for their money, people should be allowed to move it wherever they wish. Impeding its movement across borders encourages mal-investment, creating distortions in a nation's economy.

When a country's economy is in trouble—when it has a balance of trade deficit, for instance, and when its debts are mounting—and when the currency, therefore, is declining in value because everybody can see that the economy is bad, politicians, throughout history, have found a way of making things worse with the imposition of exchange controls. They run to the press and they say, "Listen, all you God-fearing Americans, Germans, Russians, whatever you are, we have a temporary problem in the financial market and it is caused by these evil speculators who are driving down the value of our currency—there is nothing wrong with our currency, we are a strong country with a sound economy, and if it were not for these speculators everything would be OK."

Diverting attention away from the real cause of the problem, which is their own mismanagement of the economy, politicians look to three crowds of people to blame for the regrettable situation. After the speculators come bankers and foreigners. Nobody likes bankers anyway, not even in good times; in bad times, everybody likes them less, because everybody sees them as rich and growing richer off the bad turn of events. Foreigners as a target are equally safe, because foreigners cannot vote. They do not have a say-so in national affairs, and remember, their food smells bad. Politicians will even blame journalists: if reporters did not write about our tanking economy, our economy would not be tanking. So we are going to enact this *temporary* measure, they say. To stem the scourge of a declining currency, we are going to make it impossible, or at least difficult, for people to take their money out of the country—it will not affect most of you because you do not travel or otherwise spend cash overseas. (See Chapter 9 and the Bernanke delusion.)

Then they introduce serious exchange controls. They are always "temporary," yet they always go on for years and years. Like anything else spawned by the government, once they are in place, a bureaucracy grows up around them. A constituency now arises whose sole purpose is to defend exchange controls and thereby assure their longevity. And they are always disastrous for a country. The free flow of capital stops. Money is trapped inside your country. And the country stops being as competitive as it once was. If you are producing tractors in the United States, say, and exchange controls are imposed, you reap an advantage from the difficulty that Americans have in getting their money out of the country to buy tractors from Germany. You and other domestic manufacturers, protected from such competition, get sloppier and sloppier, the quality of your product goes down, prices go higher and higher, and the nation's economy gets worse and worse.

The United Kingdom imposed exchange controls in 1939, and for the next forty years the country continued to deteriorate. As I pointed out earlier, not until Margaret Thatcher removed the controls in 1979 did the economy (with the help of North Sea oil) begin to improve. Currency controls more recently have constrained growth in places like China, where an inefficient allocation of capital is one cause of that country's inflation. The money has to go somewhere, and with not enough flow in and out, one of the places it has been going is into property. There has been a real estate bubble in China, which will lead to bankruptcies in the next few years.

Something like four trillion dollars' worth of foreign currencies trade every day. It is the largest market in the world. From the tourist on a package tour to Europe to people buying and selling oil around the world, all are in the currency market. There are short-term traders who are in their positions for three minutes, three hours, three days, and there are long-term investors like me.

I mainly own commodities and currencies now, and gauging the political winds, I look for more turmoil in the currency markets. For the smart investor, many more opportunities will emerge there. There are many ways to invest in currencies. You can buy futures and get enormous leverage. You can open a bank account; you can buy bonds: Swiss government bonds, for instance, in Swiss francs, or German government bonds in euros. It is now legal for American banks and brokerage firms to offer you foreign currency accounts. New instruments are becoming available. You are going to see more exchange-traded funds (ETFs) and more mutual funds invested in currencies, as Americans catch on and start putting their money abroad.

Eventually the government will react and institute exchange controls, as governments, throughout history, have always done. Washington will close down foreign currency markets for Americans, which will be a disaster, adding one more layer of grease to the skids of America's decline. But until that time, until the day bureaucrats, snarling about evil speculators and suspicious foreigners, find it politically advantageous to close the market, many more people will be investing in currencies.

In 1994, with economic problems of various kinds, China devalued its currency, setting it at a certain value against the US dollar. How smart, said Washington at the time, what geniuses these Chinese are, pegging the renminbi to the US dollar; now their economy will grow and develop in a positive way. Today, of course, Washington is shrieking at the Chinese for doing so. Those evil, filthy Communists, their economy has boomed and we are suffering, and it is all their fault for holding down the price of their currency. In 2005, the Chinese allowed some flexibility into the currency, letting it fluctuate upward a little bit, and since then it has appreciated maybe 30 percent. In a free market, it would probably have gone up more, and that is what Washington is waxing hysterical about, and in the most clueless of ways. Politicians in the United States are actually saying out loud: "We want the value of our nation's money to go down," which is what happens to the dollar when the renminbi goes up. Politicians are bashing Japan and other countries with the same line.

Now, I am an American citizen, and I do not particularly want the value of my currency to go down, but here are these elected representatives of mine screaming to debase the dollar. At the same time this is going on, little Timmy Geithner is running around saying, "We are in favor of a strong dollar." It is a mantra of the US Treasury and has been a mantra for decades, even as the national currency has been declining steadily over that time. A dollar as strong as the nation is Washington's promise to the people, yet, as soon as one of these characters goes abroad, to China, to Japan, the first thing out of his mouth is, "We want your currency to go up" (and ours to go down). The next day, it is back to basics, insisting to some reporter, "We are in favor of a strong US dollar."

The fact is that these politicians and bureaucrats, including the secretary of the Treasury, know little about currencies. They speak out of both sides of their mouths, often at the same time, and will say whatever is most politically expedient at the moment.

13

CRISIS IN PAPER MONEY

When my children were born, in addition to English and Chinese globes, I got each of them six piggy banks because I wanted them to save. They have piggy banks for various currencies. I am not trying to make currency speculators out of them, but simply trying to create awareness that there are different kinds of money and that all should be saved.

At various times in the world's history, currency exchange rates were fixed. In the nineteenth century, most currencies were fixed against gold. After the Second World War, delegates to the Bretton Woods conference fixed exchange rates around the world to the US dollar, which itself was pegged to gold, set at $35 an ounce.

When exchange rates were fixed, the value of a nation's currency was not necessarily an accurate reflection of the health of its economy. For example, after the war the deutsche mark was set at four to the dollar. Germany at the time was a destroyed nation. But the Germans rebuilt; they worked hard, saved money, and became very productive. They began building beautiful, high-quality automobiles and sold great numbers of them abroad, based on an exchange rate that had been set when the country was in ruins. Americans rushed to buy the cars because they were dirt cheap. Volkswagen, Mercedes, and BMW boomed because the deutsche mark was set at such a low rate.

For fifteen years, anything Germany sent to the United States was priced below its actual value. The country built up huge balance of trade surpluses and attracted capital. People wanted to invest in the country. German goods were of such high quality that the country wound up owning huge amounts of foreign currency reserves. The same was true of Japan, which was selling an extraordinary amount of innovative products to the United States. Normally the respective values of their currencies would have gone up. And the dollar would have declined—the United States had a ballooning balance of trade deficit. But because currency values did not adjust, pressures built up. We are in a dynamic and changing world, and anything that is artificially suppressed has a tendency to erupt out of all proportion when it is finally released. Distortions got more and more out of balance, and eventually everything popped. When Nixon finally closed the gold window in the early 1970s, the value of the dollar plunged, dramatically upsetting the world's status quo.

In the 1970s, currencies around the world started floating in value against each other. If people were bullish about sterling, it might go up in the market. Currencies could go up or down over a year or two or three; their values could adjust monthly, weekly, daily, or even hourly. If a country was getting itself into trouble, the market would undergo gradual adjustments rather than experience the abrupt crises that characterized the era of fixed rates.

We continue to have currency problems, even with floating rates, and fluctuations can be significant, in part because governments and banks continue to prop up failure. The euro, for example, is currently in crisis. Right now there are people urging a return to the gold standard. That might work for a while, but politicians have always figured out ways to get around such things, and eventually problems would resurface.

In *Adventure Capitalist* I wrote about how the Roman government added increasing amounts of base metal to its coinage through two centuries of empire. When Nero took power in Rome in A.D. 54, Roman coins were either pure silver or pure gold. By A.D. 268, silver coins consisted of only .02 percent silver, and gold coins had disappeared because smart Romans by then were hoarding gold. In fact, this is the origin of the word "debase." Franklin Roosevelt did pretty much the same thing in 1933, making it no longer legal for Americans to exchange their dollars for gold. He confiscated gold and debased the value of the dollar by almost half, raising the price of gold from $20 to $35 an ounce.

When governments run out of money, they do not stop spending. It was no different two thousand years ago than it is today. Politicians know no bounds. If Rome was running out of silver, if its economy was being mismanaged and it was running trade deficits, the only way to keep the good times rolling was to

create more money. Think of Ben Bernanke in a toga. Adulter-
ate the coinage, crank up the printing press—only the technology
changes. Governments keep running out of money, and as long
as that happens, bureaucrats and politicians will keep coming up
with ways to create it.

People throughout history have used gold, silver, copper,
bronze, seashells, ivory, cattle . . . all sorts of things . . . for money.
Gold has been used as money many times over the millennia. Silver has been used even more often. Christ was turned in for thirty
pieces of silver, not gold. The problem with any monetary system
is that politicians always figure out how to get around whatever
system is imposed, whether cash, paper money, or hard assets.
Politicians always discover ways to debase their society's money.

The only solution that would work, in my opinion, would be
to let individuals decide for themselves what to use for currency.
If you and I, when we enter into a contract, want to use seashells
as a medium of exchange, then we can use seashells, and so can
everybody else. If you and I want to use sugar to settle our affairs, fine. In that way the market would determine what money
is. Politicians would have no control over it. If the money were to
be debased, people would simply stop using it. The world would
stand on a sounder footing.

As it is, you and I cannot use anything but dollars to settle
our debts. It would be impractical for you and me to write a contract in silver, because I would have to go into the market to buy
silver, and when I gave it to you, I would have to pay a capital
gains tax on that silver. In the absence of such a monopoly money
system, politicians would founder. In the 1930s, when the United

Kingdom was in trouble, the British government made it an act of treason to use any medium of exchange other than the pound sterling. British citizens had always had a choice, so breaking mind-sets was difficult.

If we were to return to the gold standard, it would impose some discipline and stability for a while—anything right now is going to be better for a while—but the solution would be only temporary, since politicians always find ways to escape discipline. Currency crises will persist until the world goes back to a period in which the market, not the government, decides what is trustworthy as a means of exchange at any given time. Maybe all of us would use the dollar for the next three years; then somewhere along the line some of us would start using gold, or Swiss francs, or Chinese renminbi. Eventually all of us would gravitate to whatever we found to be best, or whatever the market found to be best. Right now everyone uses the US dollar, but the dollar is a very flawed currency. Some people are starting to migrate away from it, but they are not migrating as fast as they should.

Author and financial journalist Hartley Withers, a former merchant banker, addressing a meeting of the Royal Institute of International Affairs in London in 1934 on "The Future of Gold," said that "the desire for gold is a survival of primitive barbarism and dates from the time when the appeal of this nice bright metal to human vanity made it in universal demand for the adornment of the Chief, and his drinking cups, his armour, his wife and the temples of his gods," and he argued that "any article, the value of which is firmly founded on human barbarism and human stupidity, is just as impregnably founded as anything that you can conceive." And for that reason, it was a good way to guarantee the value of money. John Maynard Keynes, in 1923, in *A Tract on Monetary Reform*, wrote that the "gold standard is already a barbarous relic." Warren Buffett has dismissed it as something that "has no utility," and as "a way of going long on fear." Withers's insight, I believe, trumps all observations about gold. It (and stupidity) has outlived Keynes and will doubtless be true for even more centuries to come.

I OPENED MY first Swiss bank account in 1970. I thought I saw what was coming: continued debasement of the dollar, continued inflation. I believed that fixed exchange rates could not last. By then the pound sterling had devalued at least once, and de Gaulle was screaming about the dollar, and screaming about gold.

I went to the New York office of the Swiss Bank Corporation. This was not some retail branch down on the street corner where people deposit checks, but a big commercial bank office, and the bank officer was understandably perplexed. He was accustomed to dealing with General Motors, with people who did substantial business with Switzerland and with Europe. That is why he was in New York. And in walks this dopey little guy wanting to open up a Swiss account with the equivalent of pocket change.

I had very little money. Remember, I had just lost everything in the stock market. I was the wide-eyed Wall Street poster boy for the hazards of selling short. The bank officer wanted to be helpful, but the flight capital I was offering was such a minuscule amount that he was not about to call up Zurich. I cannot remember how I persuaded him; I told him all the reasons I had for wanting to open a Swiss account. At first he was reluctant, but eventually he let me do it. He asked where I wanted to open it; he said I had to have a branch. I told him I did not want it in the United States; I wanted a real Swiss account, where I owned Swiss francs. He would not open the account in the main office in Zurich (for fear, no doubt, that his bosses there would worry that he needed a vacation). He put me into a small retail branch in the nearby city of Winterthur. He told me it was because Winterthur was close to the Zurich airport, and that would make it convenient—if I needed that kind of convenience, now that I was a real international wheeler-dealer. You never know when you might want to go visit your fifty bucks.

Over time I continued to make investments abroad and open bank accounts abroad. It was a natural evolution. If I wanted to invest in Germany, I would open a German account, because that was obviously the best way to do it, and I always invested through the largest bank, because I figured if it got into trouble, the government would take it over, nationalize the bank, and I would not risk losing my account. Back then you could just walk in off the street. Now, of course, that is almost impossible for an American anywhere in the world. If you go into a bank, and if they allow you to open an account at all, you have to go through a comprehensive series of background and security checks. In those days you could pretty much do it over the phone. There were a couple of times where I just called up from New York. I gave my name and said I wanted to open an account, that I would fax my passport and send a check. Not anymore. Not if you are from the land of the free.

Opening the Swiss account carried me back to my university days. There were not that many Americans at Oxford when I studied there, but the few that I remember would usually sit together at lunch, and I would occasionally sit with them. Mostly they talked about politics, and I recall once saying to them that while they all aspired to be president of the United States, my plan was to be a gnome of Zurich. They thought it was very funny, but not being conversant with finance, they probably had only a vague idea what I meant.

A derogatory term for Swiss bankers—although later embraced by them with a touch of mischief—the expression "gnome of Zurich" had been coined the year I arrived in England, originating there on the political left in response to accelerating speculation against the British pound. It is attributed to the deputy leader of the Labour Party, George Brown, who emerged from a crisis meeting on the sinking currency, and announced, "The gnomes of Zurich are at it again." The reference was meant to conjure an image of the greedy little subterranean creatures of European folklore busily counting their riches in secret. Prime Minister Harold Wilson promised to resist their "sinister" power.

Some of Switzerland's more prestigious banks were established in the aftermath of the French Revolution, during the turmoil that gripped France under Napoleon. Bank people fled France and took their money over the mountains to Geneva, which was not very far away. You will see that some of the great old Swiss banks, the private banks, were founded in 1795, 1803, years like that. But by then Swiss banking traditions were already well established. Switzerland has been an international center of finance since the end of the Renaissance. Known since then for its stability, sound economy, sound currency, and privacy in financial matters, it has long provided monetary refuge for the wealthy evading the consequences of political turmoil in Europe, from French nobility fleeing the guillotine to the Jews escaping Germany a century and a half later. It has, for the same reasons, in modern times, attracted the money of numerous despots, criminal organizations, and scoundrels.

Switzerland, traditionally, has been unconditional in its offer of bank secrecy. Of course, all banks are supposed to keep your affairs quiet. If you put your money in a bank in Chicago fifty years ago, you would have done so with the assumption that it was confidential. In America, as we have seen, that is no longer the case. The government can look into your bank account, your bedroom, your mail . . . anywhere it wants. And in much the way that our privacy has been taken away from us, the Swiss have recently surrendered some of theirs, succumbing to pressure from the United States. Bank secrecy in Switzerland is not as sacrosanct as it once was.

Nonetheless, the first thing people look for when seeking monetary refuge is safety. They want stability. They want the security of knowing they will get their money back, and that they will get back at least as much as they put there in the first place. That depends entirely on a sound currency. And that is something the Swiss franc has always offered. The question, now, is whether that is going to last.

I had opened my account in 1970 in the face of coming turmoil in the currency markets. By the end of the decade, as the markets grew more volatile, people all over the world were trying to open Swiss accounts. And the same thing is happening today. The dollar is suspect, the euro is suspect, and again people are rushing to the franc. In 2011, the CHF (the Swiss franc) escalated to record highs against both the euro and the dollar, rising 43 percent against the euro in a year and a half as of August 2011. It was a "massive overvaluation," according to the country's central bank, the Swiss National Bank (SNB). Under pressure from the country's exporters, the SNB announced that "the value of the franc is a threat to the economy" and said it was "prepared to purchase foreign exchange in unlimited quantities" in order to drive the price down.

A threat to the economy? It was the exporters who were doing the screaming, but everybody else in Switzerland was better-off. When the franc rises, everything the Swiss import goes down in price, whether it is cotton shirts, TVs, or cars. The standard of living for everybody goes up. Every citizen of Switzerland benefits from a stronger currency. Our dental technician down in Geneva is not calling up and moaning. She is happy. Everything she buys is cheaper. But the big exporters get on the phone and the government takes their call.

The franc went down 7 or 8 percent the day of the SNB announcement. Nobody, at least in the beginning, wanted to take on the central bank. But the bank's currency manipulation will turn out to be disastrous. One of two things is going to happen.

In the first scenario, the market will continue to buy Swiss francs, which means that the Swiss National Bank will just have to keep printing and printing and printing, and that will of course

debase the currency. Now, there are major exporters in Switzerland who might benefit, but the largest industry in Switzerland,
the single largest business, is finance. The economy rises or falls
on the nation's ability to attract capital. And the reason people put
their money there is their trust in the soundness of the currency—
they know that their money will be there when they want it, and
that it will not be worth significantly less than when they put it
there in the first place. But people will stop rushing to put their
money into a country where the value of the currency is deliber-
ately being driven down. After the Second World War and for the
next thirty years, people took their money out of the United Kingdom because the currency plummeted. (Politicians blamed it on
the gnomes of Zurich.) London ceased to be the world's reserve
financial center because Britain's money was no good. Similarly,
if you debase the franc, eventually nobody will want it. You will
have eroded its value, not simply as a medium of exchange, but
also as a monetary refuge. The money will move to Singapore or
Hong Kong, and the Swiss finance industry will wither up and
disappear.

The alternative scenario is what happened in July 2010, the
last time the Swiss tried to weaken their currency. They did so by
buying up foreign currencies to hold against the franc—selling
the franc to keep the price down. But the market just kept buying the francs, and the Swiss central bank, after quadrupling its
foreign currency holdings, abandoned the effort. At that point,
when the bank stopped selling it, the Swiss franc rose in value,
all the currencies the Swiss had bought (and were now holding)
declined in value, and the country lost $21 billion. In the end, the

market had more money than the bank, and market forces inevitably prevailed.

In the late 1970s when everyone was rushing to the franc, the Swiss National Bank, to stem the tide, imposed negative interest rates on foreign depositors. The government levied a tax on anybody who bought the currency. It was their form of exchange controls back then. If you bought 100 Swiss francs, you wound up with 70 in your pocket. The other 30 went to pay the tax. Today, with the rush on again, *The Economist* has described the Swiss currency as an "innocent bystander in a world where the eurozone's politicians have failed to sort out their sovereign-debt crisis, America's economic policy seems intent on spooking investors and the Japanese have intervened to hold down the value of the yen."

All of which is true, but I think the problem runs deeper than that. The Swiss for decades have had a semimonopoly on finance. And as a result they have become less and less competent. The entire economy has been overprotected. The reason Swiss Air went bankrupt is because it never really had to compete. Any monopoly eventually destroys itself, and Switzerland, in predictable fashion, is corroding from within. As a result, other financial centers have been rising: London, Lichtenstein, Vienna, Singapore, Dubai, Hong Kong.

I still have those original Swiss francs that I bought in 1970, and since then the franc is up about 400 percent. Granted, it has been over forty years, but 400 percent is nothing to sneeze at. Plus I have been collecting interest. Had I kept the money in an American savings account, it would have gone down 80 percent against the franc.

. . .

PAIGE AND I, on our Millennium Adventure, passed through Western Europe in the fall of 1999, coming out of Russia, and spent three and a half months there in advance of our marriage. Had it not been for the wedding, we would have set out for Africa much sooner. Spending the extra time there, however, proved beneficial. I was able to fine-tune my position on the European Union's adoption of a single currency, the euro.

I had felt from the outset that the world needed something like the euro badly. The world's central banks held about 60 percent of their foreign currency reserves in dollars. I believed the dollar to be seriously flawed, and the prospect of the euro's replacing it as the chief reserve currency and medium of exchange offered what appeared to be a solution. The European Union's economy and population are larger than those of the United States, so it has the size and depth necessary to support a world currency, in addition to which, unlike the United States, it does not, overall, have a big balance of trade deficit. In late 1999, when I was in Europe, at the end of the currency's first year in existence, it was estimated that, were the currency to succeed, 30 percent of the world's trade would be denominated in euros.

By then, however, I did not, and I do not now, expect the euro to survive as we now know it.

The euro, which resulted from the Maastricht Treaty of 1992, was officially instituted on January 1, 1999. Notes and coins began circulating in 2002. It was intended as a strong currency, modeled on those of Germany, the Netherlands, and Luxembourg, whose economies were also strong. Those three countries, Germany being dominant, along with Belgium, France, and Italy, whose economies and currencies were weaker, made up the Inner Six founding member states of the European Communities. When the euro was finally adopted, all members of the eurozone—today there are seventeen of them—agreed to run their economies on the German model. Not even the Germans seem to have succeeded.

The Maastricht Treaty stipulated that no member government could run a deficit of more than 3 percent in any one year. The French, in order to abide by the contract, were the first to institute phony bookkeeping. *We will not pay our pension obligations this year, we will pay them next year,* they decided. *This year things will look good, next year things will look worse, but next year is next year and we are not going to worry about that.* It is the Scarlett O'Hara theory of finance: "After all . . . tomorrow is another day." The move was seen as pretty outrageous. Even the Italians, who had been using phony bookkeeping for decades—for centuries, in fact—were shocked. After pulling themselves up off the floor, they proceeded to emulate the French, going with their own time-honored recipe for cooking the books.

Everybody hurls bricks at the Greeks right now, but by the late 1990s, everybody was fudging the accounts to abide by the terms of the treaty.

Soon, most of the countries just went ahead and ignored the treaty altogether. They did not even bother to pretend. Who could care less about the contract? All the guys who originally signed the agreement—the ones who appreciated that a sound currency relied necessarily on strong economies—were either dead or long retired. The new guys were preoccupied with being reelected, the demands of which were not well served by ridiculous fantasies like fiscal discipline.

Right now, under any regimen, it will be impossible for many countries to pay off their debts. Ever. It is not going to happen. So, accepting that, what should Europe do? My solution is the one the market has been imposing for thousands of years. Let them default. Let them go bankrupt. The people who are in debt with them, either by lending to them or investing with them, will take losses, serious losses in some cases, but then, for example, Greece can start over from a sound base. The country need not leave the eurozone to do it. We in America have had states go bankrupt, counties, cities—Mississippi did not pull out of the United States because it went bankrupt. Neither did New York, nor did Detroit. They went through a period of pain, people lost money, wages went down, rents went down, haircuts went down, everything went down as people adjusted to the reality that they did not have any money, that they could no longer spend money they did not have, and that nobody would lend them any money. But they prevailed. And nowhere along the way did the US dollar disappear.

Unfortunately, politicians in Greece or somewhere else will see pulling out of the euro as the easy solution. *The hell with the euro, we will go back to the drachma!* And that would be a mistake. There may be a burst of enthusiasm at the beginning. Everybody will have this new drachma, and things may look OK for a while. But the optimism will not last. A return to the drachma will just serve as a license for the government to print money, and for the

Greeks to continue spending money they do not have. The drachma will trade at such a low price that the country will enjoy a much-improved balance of trade, but everybody's net worth will have collapsed. Nobody will trust the currency, or the Greeks themselves. Nobody will lend them money. Nobody will invest there.

There is no scenario under consideration, there is no scenario possible, that alters the fact that over the next few decades people are not going to be living great lives in Greece. And all those people who loaned Greece money are going to take big losses. If Angela Merkel could get all of them into a room and say, "OK, *this* bank is going to close, *that* bank is going to stay in business, *this* guy is going to be out of a job . . . all you guys are going to take hits, but we are going to hold everything together, everybody's savings are safe, checks will clear, depositors' money will be protected, we will ring-fence the banks, the system is not going to freeze up and close down," it might be different. If the chancellor of Germany could do that, the market would buy it, because at the moment governments in Europe have enough money. And they have enough credibility. If it happens five years from now, she can drag them all into a room, talk to them all day long, and nobody will notice. The problem will be so bad by then that you are looking at systemic failure—the market says the hell with all of you, and the whole system collapses.

And, in my view, that is exactly what will happen, because politicians do not have the brains or the courage to take the necessary steps. None of them is talking about bailing out the Greeks. It is all about bailing out the banks, bailing out the management of the banks, the stockholders of the banks, and the bondholders of the banks who invested in Greece. The people of Greece will suffer, but the banks will survive: the CEOs will make their salaries, the shareholders will get their dividends, the bondholders will survive. Greeks will be out on the street, unemployed. They will be there either way. The difference is that my way things eventually get better, as has happened in Iceland since 2009; the other way, everything just gets worse.

14

NO ONE HAS EVER REPEALED THE LAWS OF SUPPLY AND DEMAND

The world is going to see higher prices for food in the near future, in part because inventories are so low around the globe. If nature does not cooperate —if, for example, it does not rain in Brazil— there will be fewer inventories to fall back on, and prices will go even higher. Politicians will blame the increase on evil specula- tors, but the facts are that if prices do not go higher, farmers will bring in no new production. If the poor wheat farmer is sitting there saying, "Well, I can only sell my wheat at $3," he is not going to produce wheat that costs him $4 to grow (or whatever the numbers happen to be). But if the price goes to $8, all the wheat farmers in the world, and even some who are not wheat farmers, are going to run out to produce it.

In the meantime, you and I will be irritated by the high cost of bread. But if we did not pay so much for bread, we would not get *any* bread. That is the way the world has worked for thousands of years. The Communists of the former Soviet Union tried to override the laws of supply and demand, and the result was that they did not have access to anything. Shortages were an everyday fact of life. In Russia, people would spend two or three hours a day standing in line, trying to get tomatoes, trying to get almost anything. You would walk out onto the street and if you saw a line of people outside a shop, you would get in it, regardless of what was for sale. The line meant that something had come into that shop, and whatever it was, you wanted to get your hands on it. Even if you had no use for it, if you happened to be male, for example, and it was something like women's clothing, you would get in line to buy it—you knew you could eventually swap whatever it was, trading with somebody else for something you needed.

People who have tried to outmaneuver the marketplace have never succeeded. No pope, no imam, has the power to negate the laws of supply and demand. But that will not stop politicians. Sometime in the near future you will see them institute price controls. Politicians have been doing it for a thousand years, and they continue to do it, even though it never has worked. Politicians in the Philippines capped the price of rice a few years ago. The farmers stopped farming. Filipinos kept eating rice—it was the cheapest thing around—and as the price of corn and wheat went up, they continued to eat even more rice. Discouraging production and increasing consumption had the predictable result. Eventually there was little rice. It wasn't profitable to produce it. The policy quickly ended.

In the late 1890s, with the price of wheat going up, politicians in Germany, in an attempt to curb "evil speculators," passed a law making it illegal to trade wheat on a commodity exchange. The price of wheat then skyrocketed; politicians, to their credit, realized their mistake, and they abolished the law after three years. But in the United States in the 1950s, under comparable circumstances, Congress passed a similar law pertaining to onions. And the law persists. In America today, onions are the only commodity that it is illegal to trade on a futures exchange. As soon as the law was passed, the price of onions doubled, and in the past decade onions went up in price more than any other food, so high in price, in fact, that India imposed price controls.

The Soviets did not have anything because nobody produced anything, and nobody produced anything because prices were set so low. When I was driving through Russia on my motorcycle trip, kids were using loaves of bread for footballs. The price of bread was set at an artificially low level, and it was cheaper to buy a succession of loaves than it was to buy a football (if you could find one to buy), so there they were, out in the street, kicking loaves of bread around. Kvass, made from fermented bread, was far and away the most common beverage in the USSR. Bread was dirt cheap, but it meant the people had nothing else. The Filipinos and the Germans learned quickly that price controls were destined to fail. The Soviets did not catch on until the whole place just fell apart.

The International Energy Agency has said that the world's known reserves of oil are declining at the rate of 6 percent a year, and that is after discoveries. That means that, barring new discoveries or widespread success with extracting processes like fracking, in sixteen years there will be no oil at any price. Fortunately, fracking is having at least short-term success in helping extend supply. Serious supply problems like this are what have led to the bull market in commodities, and prices are going to go much higher.

And instability will follow.

If the price of copper goes up, not many people know it right away. But if the prices of wheat and sugar go up, everybody knows it that day, and everybody is unhappy that day. And that often leads to social unrest. Tunisia, Egypt, Libya, Yemen, Syria . . . they are just the beginning. With rising food prices worldwide we are going to see more discontent, we are going to see more governments collapse, we are going to see more countries disintegrate.

In my book *Adventure Capitalist*, I wrote of driving through Egypt with Paige:

"We learned why the government of Hosni Mubarak is hated in the streets. The government has spies everywhere and strangles any initiative or dissent. . . . Mubarak remains in power only because of the United States, and the anger at him is so widespread that whether he is overthrown or just dies, there will eventually be turmoil in the largest country in the Middle East. . . . If you fly to Cairo, get taxied over to the pyramids, and then take a bus down to Luxor, you see none of this."

That was in the fall of 2000. Mubarak was ousted in the popular uprising that swept Egypt in 2011. You have these long-entrenched dictators whose people now have access to the Internet, to a variety of social media, to endless streams of information and to instant communication for the purposes of political organizing. And the people are taking their discontent onto the streets. But the spark igniting the activity is not necessarily political so much as it is economic: surging inflation, high unemployment, and an escalating cost of living, most significantly a rise in food prices. These are the things that make people deeply angry. (The Tiananmen Square protests in Beijing in the spring of 1989 started out as protests against inflation and rising prices. Not until the Western press showed up did students start shouting words like "democracy.") Egyptians do not really care whether Hillary Clinton, the US secretary of state, champions them as politically downtrodden, especially since America was the regime's main support for decades. They do care if the price of bread skyrockets and there is nothing they can do about it. They do care if they cannot find a job.

It is happening in the Middle East, and it is going to happen in other countries, as well. We see it in various places in Europe and are beginning to see it in the United States. Not for the first time.

In March 1894, which was the second year of the worst economic depression the United States had experienced up to that time, a wealthy Massillon, Ohio, businessman named Jacob S. Coxey organized a march on Washington to protest government inaction in the face of the crisis, and to lobby the US Congress to allocate funds to create a vast program of public works. At the height of the four-year depression, which was prompted by the Panic of 1893, up to one-fifth of the nation's workforce would be unemployed. Before it ended, some fifteen thousand businesses would fail, including more than five hundred banks and a good share of the nation's railroads, among them the Union Pacific, the Northern Pacific, and the Atchison, Topeka & Santa Fe.

"Coxey's Army," as it came to be known, was one of several groups of unemployed workers, numbering in the thousands, that set out from all over the country that spring, and it was the only group to reach the nation's capital. Arriving on May 1, Coxey and his five hundred marchers were set upon by police, beaten with nightsticks, and driven from the lawn of the Capitol building, from where Coxey intended to give a speech. The marchers dispersed, Coxey and his lieutenants were arrested, and Coxey spent twenty days in jail, held on the only charge available to the government: stepping on the Capitol grass.

Thirty-eight years later, in 1932, a Roman Catholic priest in Pittsburgh named James Renshaw Cox led twenty-five thousand unemployed Pennsylvanians—known as "Cox's Army"—in a march on Washington, similarly to lobby Congress to create a public works program. It was the largest demonstration in the nation's capital up to that time. Cox ran that year as the first presidential candidate of the Jobless Party, pulling out two months before the election to throw his support behind Franklin D. Roosevelt.

In Jacob Coxey's 1894 speech, which was read into the *Congressional Record* eight days after his arrest, Coxey quoted an unnamed US senator who argued "that for a quarter of a century the rich have been growing richer, the poor poorer, and that by the close of the present century the middle class will have disappeared as the struggle for existence becomes fierce and relentless."

Sound familiar? The recent movement that calls itself Occupy Wall Street is reading from the same playbook. And we have not seen the end of such protests.

Now, I take issue with the movement's reasoning. Their claim is that 1 percent of the population owns too much of the nation's wealth. My response is to say that 50 percent of the people in America pay no federal income taxes at all, and attacking the 50 percent who do pay taxes does not seem to me to be the way to solve the problem. At least some people are working, saving and investing, paying taxes and creating jobs.

"Let not him who is houseless pull down the house of another," said Abraham Lincoln, "but let him labor diligently and build one for himself, thus by example assuring that his own shall be safe from violence when built."

To those activists who vilify billionaires, I would point out some simple arithmetic. According to a list that was recently compiled by one institutional trading firm, forty-two of the publicly traded US companies founded by billionaires employ a collective total of more than four million people globally.

In the mid-1960s, in the United Kingdom, Prime Minister Harold Wilson's cabinet was considering the steps that would be necessary to build a national semiconductor industry. This took place at a time when computers and semiconductors were the wave of the future. The cabinet decided against moving forward with a plan because, as one minister explained it, "if we develop a semiconductor industry some people are going to get very rich, and it is not our policy to create millionaires." And, of course, a decade later the United Kingdom was bankrupt.

There comes a time in every country's, company's, family's, or individual's life when it becomes necessary to deal with past mistakes. Recessions are endemic to our nation's economy. Every four to six years we have a slowdown. We are in the midst of a recession now. But the government is mishandling it, refusing to address earlier mistakes. What is going to happen the next time, or if not the next time, the time after that? America has shot its wad. The next time around, our problems are going to be worse, since the debt will be so, so much higher. There are going to be that many more people in the street, screaming and pleading, and the nation will have lost the financial wherewithal to address their grievances.

THROUGHOUT THE WORLD, because of commodities shortages, we are going to see a rise of social unrest—it is happening, and getting worse—and the governments that are most vulnerable are those in the grip of these thirty-year-long dictatorships.

Which raises the question of China. You hear politicians in America railing about China's Communist dictatorship. Which dictatorship would that be? What dictator? What is his name? The Chinese government changes automatically every five years, and no leader can serve more than two consecutive terms. That is hardly a dictatorship.

Becoming a Chinese leader is the result of a thorough and very rigorous process. You really have to be vetted. You have to spend thirty or forty years working your way up through the ranks, being tested all along. There are millions of people in the Communist Party, and its general secretary is selected by consensus following years of preparation during which a candidate must prove himself. In some ways it is better than the US system, where a guy with money who is good on TV can be president with little more than the right suit and hairstyle.

General Secretary Hu Jintao, who also held the position of president, stepped down from the former position in 2012 and resigns the latter in 2013. As does the premier of the state council, with whom he has shared power, Wen Jiabao. All three offices carry the burden of accountability. The gibberish about a dictatorship smacks of lunacy to anyone who has done his homework. China has not had a dictator since the death of Mao Zedong. Vladimir Putin of Russia is a dictator. He wields much more power than anybody in China today. That kind of power is unavailable within the constraints of the Chinese system. I am not saying that theirs is the best system, but I know it certainly has worked in China. The country's success is evidence of that.

When I first went to China thirty years ago, there was one radio station, one TV station, one newspaper, one way to dress. Many media outlets exist now in China, and millions of people are on the Internet. Demonstrations occur in the streets every week. (The Chinese government said there were 110,000 demonstrations in 2010.) People are demanding what they feel they are owed, whether rising up against a crooked landlord or denouncing some official for bureaucratic corruption. And the protests are making the press. You cannot hide these things now. Not in the twenty-first century. The leadership is held accountable. The government is putting bureaucrats in jail, and in some cases even executing them, in response to the resentment of the populace. In

December 2011, in the village of Wukan, in southern Guangdong Province, villagers held a large demonstration, and they threw the local government out. They held an election and did things the way they wanted to do them. So China has changed a lot. It is not yet the Netherlands, or like other wide-open nations, but it is certainly opening up. The process unquestionably has its flaws, but so does our system of politics. Ours is a far less rigorous system, and it shows in the caliber of our leadership: Clinton, Bush, Obama . . . Could it be any worse?

Chinese leaders voluntarily give up their power after a certain number of years, and they pass it on to carefully selected, rigorously vetted successors. I am sure Confucius would have approved wholeheartedly. He authored the texts in which the scholar-bureaucrats, or mandarins, were schooled, the classics upon which the imperial examination was based. If you proved to be skilled and smart and knowledgeable, you attained a position of leadership. For centuries, China has administered nationwide examinations. The country has a long history of respect and admiration for scholarship. I do not know if that makes it the best system, but it is certainly different from what we have.

Many Asians say that the Asian Way is first to open up your economy, to bring prosperity to your country, and then, only after that, to open up your political system. They say that the reason the Russians failed is that they did it the other way around. Russia opened up its political system in the absence of a sound economy, everybody bitched and complained, and chaos inevitably ensued. As examples of the Asian path to political openness, they point to

South Korea and Taiwan, both of which were once vicious dictatorships supported by the United States. Japan was at one time a one-party state supported by the US military. Singapore achieved its current status under one-party, authoritarian rule. All these countries have since become more prosperous and more open.

Plato, in *The Republic*, says that the way societies evolve is by going from dictatorship to oligarchy to democracy to chaos and back to dictatorship. It has a certain logic, and Plato was a very smart guy. I do not know if the Asians ever read *The Republic*, but the Asian Way seems to suggest that Plato knew whereof he spoke.

Not only is the Asian model different from that of the Soviets, it stands China in marked contrast to those thirty-year dictatorships previously mentioned. Chinese leaders have put a high premium upon changing the country's economy, presumably to seek prosperity for the 1.3 billion people who live there. When we look to the Middle East, we do not see a lot of leaders with similar priorities. Dictators there are taking money and throwing it into Swiss bank accounts, ready to blow town on a moment's notice, at whatever point in the future it becomes necessary to flee. Their priorities are to reward their families, reward their friends, and get a lot of money outside the country secretly.

Yes, some Chinese are doing the same thing. Corruption exists in China as it does everywhere, including the United States. It is endemic to human beings, whether Chinese or African or American. But when the Chinese expose corruption, they are pretty brutal about it. Perpetrators are usually jailed or executed, and executed pretty quickly. According to Xinhua, the state news agency, more than 880,000 party members were punished from 2003 to 2008, which is in sharp contrast to the West, where very few in government or commerce have been punished for abusing the system. At least in China those in a position to benefit from corruption leave office every five years, making way for a different crowd to come along and do the same; at least there is some turnover.

THE CIVIL UPRISINGS that constitute what is known as the Arab Spring are unlikely, it seems to me, to lead to a reflowering of the culture that made the Middle East the cradle of civilization. Medicine, physics, astronomy, mathematics . . . all of it came out of the Arab world. While Europeans emerging from caves were still painting themselves blue, Arabs were creating the alphabet and giving the world such things as algebra and celestial navigation. Today the only force in the region that seems to be politically organized has as its aspiration a revival of fundamentalist Islam. America, which supported dictatorships in Tunisia, Egypt, and Yemen while paying lip service to a desire for freedom in those countries, is not going to be happy with what it is getting. Rather than a shift that is pro-democracy, we will see one that is anti-American, anti-Israel. In hard times, as I said before, everybody looks for scapegoats. The scapegoats are usually foreigners, and in the Middle East the traditional, historic scapegoat has been the United States.

In the thirty years that Mubarak was dictator in Egypt, China rocketed forward economically. Egypt progressed not at all. The Middle East has seen little economic return, or change of any kind. With tangible economic change, people are less likely to grow angry. If they are eating well, if they have a house and a car, they are less likely to go into the streets. That was the genius of Singapore. One of the government's first priorities was to get everybody his own home, one in which he could take pride. From the very beginning, the government began tearing down slums and building HDB flats. If you had your own house, there was not that much urgency to go out and join the Communist Party or become active in a trade union. You were participating in the growth of the economy.

In parts of Asia, prosperity is evident, and in some places prosperity has been a precursor to democracy. In Singapore it will be interesting to see if prosperity leads its beneficiaries to take on the government. The old-timers remember how tough things used to be in the early days, and how effectively the government has improved their economic prospects since then, while immigrants like us know how bad it is in other places. The subsequent generation has known only the good times. Everybody under forty grew up prosperous, and it is they who rail about multiparty democracy. This happened in Taiwan, it happened in South Korea, and it happened in Japan. Young people achieve success, and they want to be able to change the government, just the way Plato said. There is nothing new about it.

It is sure to happen eventually in China. The country faces a difficult challenge in bringing prosperity to a vast and widely dispersed population outside the major cities. But the government has proved quick on its feet. Mao Zedong's Cultural Revolution and the Great Leap Forward were the nadir of a few hundred years of decline at the end of which everything precipitously collapsed. Within two years of Mao's death, under Deng Xiaoping, a range of positive changes was under way. In November 1978, Deng visited, among other places, Singapore, where he met with Prime Minister Lee Kuan Yew. It was Singapore that helped provide a model for the reforms instituted in China and for the latter's move to a market economy. By 1990, China had a real stock exchange. The reason the country is booming today is the unleashing of entrepreneurship. People can do what they want. Yes, there was central planning; yes, there were government companies; yes, yes, yes to all that. But what some see as socialism-with-a-Chinese-face is simply a vestige, a reflection of the fact that for thirty years everything in China was owned by the state. What you are looking at in China today is capitalism.

The Chinese are among the best capitalists in the world. California is more Communist than China. Massachusetts is more socialist than China. I have run into many businesspeople who love doing business in China, because once they get approval to go forward, they are left pretty much unfettered. And getting approval is not that hard. Of course, there are constraints and there are horror stories. But for the most part these people would rather do business in China than just about anywhere else in the world, including South Korea, including Europe, and certainly including the United States.

15

THE SUN IS RISING IN THE EAST

Pundits pontificating in the press take great pleasure in predicting that China is headed for a hard landing or even a collapse, faced as it is with having to maintain what they see as an unsustainable growth rate. The numbers they throw about are 8 percent, 7.5 percent. First of all, every country, including the United States, wants to sustain a high growth rate. Without a high growth rate, all politicians would suffer. Second, but more important, the numbers you get out of any government are nothing more than a mirage.

All the growth-rate figures are unreliable. It is stupefying to me that India could claim to have a clue what is going on even in India, much less in China or in the United States. America is always revising its numbers, and most of them are made up. I have learned over the years not to pay any attention to them. They are mainly exercises in public relations.

When it comes to growth rate, the Indians base their numbers on what China is reporting, making sure that theirs are better than, or at least in line with, China's. All this talk about how much China has, or has not, been growing is propaganda. What I know is that every time I go there I see that something real is happening. And what I learn by actually going there is all I really need to know.

That having been said, there is nothing to prevent China from experiencing a recession. Leaders are doing their best to keep their growth rate up, and in recent years they have done a better job than most countries in managing their economy. But no matter how smart they are, they are still bureaucrats, and that makes a recession not merely possible, but probable. China is going to have plenty of setbacks. Anybody who thinks otherwise has just not read his history and does not understand how the world works. So, yes, let us suppose that China has a recession. What is the worst that happens—they throw out the Communists?

With regularity, in the decades following the Second World War, a great hullabaloo would rise out of Washington, with red-baiting politicians fulminating about who lost China. In a few years, we will see a variation on the red scare as the same kinds of people go nuts, asking how the Chinese came to have everything and the United States was left out in the cold. The answer is that they did it by being great capitalists. They continue to seek out opportunities in the world and exploit them, which is what capitalists do.

The Chinese are going around the globe and buying up all sorts of productive assets, oil fields, plantations, mines, everything they can find, because they see what I see, and that is a shortage of raw materials. And they are making many friends doing it. Their method stands in sharp contrast to that of the United States and the old colonial powers of Europe, who went in and essentially took things by force, paying well below value when they paid anything at all, while pushing people around and telling them how to live and whom to worship.

Nobody objects to the way the Chinese do business. They boss nobody around. They show up with money and say, "Let's make a deal. The deal you need is the deal we need." They make the deal, everybody is happy, and then they go away. No propaganda. "This is strictly business, folks, nothing else. Not like the old days."

In Africa they are very popular because they pay top dollar. Chinese leaders have visited nearly every country in Africa in the past decade or so. They bring Africa to China—hosting huge events at which the leaders of more than fifty African countries show up. Only two or three times in history has an American president touched down anywhere on the African continent.

The Chinese are doing the same thing in South America and Central Asia. They buy whatever they can. They are making enormous inroads, locking down minerals and other raw materials, while other countries, including the United States, appear to ignore or be blind to the fact that the world is running short of them. The Chinese are anticipating. They are out in the world reacting to what they see coming. They are acting the part of the good capitalist while America acts like the arrogant superpower of the 1950s, the postwar period in which the country did not have to worry about a thing.

Those days, of course, are long gone. It has just not sunk in.

Spending money, without any arm-twisting, and to some extent providing jobs, China generates goodwill and gains political influence. To the same end, the Chinese have talked about buying European government bonds, with everybody in Europe currently being in trouble. Now for the Chinese point of view: Let us assume the Chinese never get their money back, out of Greece or Portugal or wherever. Let us say they lose money. From the Chinese point of view, it is cheap foreign aid, cheap influence peddling, a cheap price to pay for power on the international stage. Even if the worst happens, even if China loses its investment, it will gain political leverage, at the IMF, at the World Bank. The Chinese rode to our rescue, the Europeans will say. They were the good guys; they bought our bonds when nobody else would or could.

America might like to buy the bonds, but America does not have the money, a case where being overextended redounds to our disadvantage once again as even the US Defense Department studies show.

PAIGE AND I recently returned from a visit to Myanmar, a country that shows all the signs of being America's next missed opportunity.

In 1962, Myanmar, then known as Burma, was the richest country in Asia. That is when the first general, the numerologist Ne Win, took power, initiating fifty years of military rule. Since then astrologers and numerologists have been running the country. Ne Win and his successors, ushering in a Soviet-style economic program, the Burmese Way to Socialism, closed off the country, and then, of course, Myanmar—as it was officially renamed in 1989—became one of the poorest countries in the world.

Now in transition to civilian rule, Myanmar today, after suffering half a century of mismanagement, stagnation, and isolation, is where Deng Xiaoping's China was in 1978. Its economy is one of the least developed. And there is not a more exciting investment opportunity that I can think of—sixty million people, huge natural resources, with a highly educated, disciplined workforce, nestled between India and China. I wanted very much to invest there, but the restrictions were so onerous that it might actually have been easier for me to invest in North Korea—more about that later—not because Myanmar made it onerous, but because America did. I had my lawyer look into it, and it is all but criminal for an American even to say the word "Myanmar." I went through the charade of applying for a license from the government, my government, the US government, which would have allowed me to invest in Myanmar, but nothing happened, as I expected.

The rest of the world is pouring into Myanmar, right behind the rest of Asia, which is already there. The British, whose rule during the colonial period transformed what was once a feudal society, are pretty much unrestricted there. It is really only we, in the land of the free, who were prevented from participating in the great changes taking place. Those who were not there yet were racing to get there as fast as they could, because they knew that for a while they would not have to compete with the United

States. If you were in the oil business, and you did not have to compete with Exxon, you would hurry too. By the time Americans were finally free to join the rush, others had already bought up a lot of the good stuff.

Again, it is just one more example of American shortsightedness. Even in Iran, where I invested some twenty years ago, you could get a US license allowing you to invest, as long as you did not invest over X million dollars. But when it comes to Myanmar, as I read it, and as my lawyer read it, just going there bordered on a crime for an American citizen, as far as the US government was concerned.

For Paige and me, traveling on simple tourist visas acquired in Singapore, our recent visit was our second. We had driven through the country ten years earlier, in 2001, on our Millennium Adventure. On this trip, as on our first, we met a lot of people. I met with various bank presidents and mining people to discuss the changes happening in Myanmar, and everybody seemed convinced that the changes were real. I met with the head of the Chamber of Commerce. Until a few months before, the position had been filled by a government appointee. This man was elected by Chamber members.

"I have to keep the members happy now, or I won't keep my job," he explained.

Paige is now an aspiring gemologist. Having already acquired various certifications, she is studying all the time, taking tests all the time, and while we were in Myanmar, which is a rich source of sapphires, rubies, and jade, she furthered her education. A friend introduced her to a well-connected Burmese woman who knew everybody in Yangon. Knowing of Paige's interest in gemstones, she came calling with stones from several dealers. Paige found herself, at one point, with $15 million to $20 million worth of colorful jewels arrayed before her to study. She was in heaven.

One night, invited to dinner, I was seated next to the head of a large travel agency, and I told him about our drive through Myanmar in 2001. He said that such a trip was not possible. It would not have been allowed in 2001, he advised me, nor would it be allowed today. I agreed with him that it could not have been done, neither back then nor now, "but we did it," I said. And I directed him to our website for evidence of the trip. He was flabbergasted, to my delight, as you can imagine. His disbelief at what we had done just served to reinforce how complicated and unusual it was and made the memory of the accomplishment that much sweeter.

In 2001, at the time of our first visit, numerous countries were doing business in Myanmar: Japan, China, India, Malaysia, Russia, Singapore. These nations were poised to exploit a variety of natural resources—timber, natural gas, gold and other minerals—and to capitalize on what we saw as the inevitable growth of tourism. In Delhi, a month before our visit, we met an American woman who was heading there, and who grew indignant when I mentioned that we would be there, too, claiming that US sanctions prohibited our going.

"Why can you go and I can't?" I asked her.

"Because I work for an NGO," she said, a nongovernmental organization. "I'm going to Myanmar to examine the situation."

"So am I" was my answer. "Why should I let you go to Myanmar, examine the situation, and make a judgment for me?"

(For my opinion, in more depth, of the foreign-aid scam that is nongovernmental organizations and the expatriate Americans who gravitate to them, see *Adventure Capitalist*.)

Wherever we went in Myanmar in 2001, wherever we went in the world in the course of our three-year trip, we found that US sanctions were ineffective. Competing products swept in, or American products were smuggled in. Either way, it was not the "offending" countries, but American workers, businesses, and taxpayers who were the losers. Today, as we discovered on our more recent trip, you can still get anything you want in Myanmar. An additional decade of sanctions has had little success.

Following the installation of a new government, and the promise of democratic reforms, the United States was finally one of the last to announce easing of sanctions. Let us hope they stay eased.

Meanwhile, Myanmar, which will host the Southeast Asian Games in 2013, has been chosen to assume the rotating chairmanship of the Association of Southeast Asian Nations (ASEAN) in 2014. All its neighbors are keen on what is happening.

The country instituted a new currency system. The system they had was out of control, and the IMF helped them figure out what to do about it. Myanmar has been a cash society. No credit cards, few checks. I visited some banks, and I have never seen anything quite like it, and I have been to a lot of places: you go into the bank, you look over the counter, and you see a small room filled with cash, stacked to the ceiling.

When we were there (in the summer of 2011), the official exchange rate in Myanmar was 6 kyat to the dollar. The black market rate was 800 to the dollar. But the black market rate the year before was 50 percent higher, 1,200 to the dollar. The black market knows what I know: that things are opening up and changing for the better. The black market and the currency markets are frequently among the first to know. They already see what is happening.

Even in 2012 in Myanmar you could not use a credit card, so huge changes are coming between now and the opening of the Southeast Asian Games. You cannot invite people from nine other nations to come to your country and not allow them to charge. And you cannot institute a credit-card system with an out-of-control currency. Myanmar recognized the problem; it knew the currency problem had to be solved first. Tourists are not going to come and use credit cards to charge things on the black market. And they will not come if you do not offer them a place to stay. There will be new hotels and restaurants, and by necessity, there will be credit cards.

IN 2007, Paige and I received permission to visit North Korea. I wanted to go there because I sensed that changes were coming. I wanted to see what I could see. We spent four days there as tourists. Paige at the time was a few months pregnant with Baby Bee.

I am not a tour group kind of person. I like to make my own way and create my own itinerary, to decide where to go and what to eat. That is not an option in North Korea, where we had government minders every minute we were there. Walking down the main thoroughfare in Pyongyang, I saw a barbershop, and because I needed a haircut, I ducked inside, where an old man sitting on a stool stood up in shock when I started pantomiming the use of scissors with my hands. I was summarily pulled outside by one of our minders. A haircut, he assured me, was not on the agenda.

By 2007, I think, only something like three hundred Americans had been to North Korea since before the Second World War—there was some strange statistic like that. Virtually no Americans had been allowed to go there since General Douglas MacArthur's troops went across in the early 1950s.

It was clear to me that the North Koreans knew that their country needed changing. And it was not hard to understand why. All the North Korean generals, as young officers, thirty years ago, were sent to places like Beijing, Moscow, and Shanghai. Today they go as generals and see the changes that have taken place, and when they return to Pyongyang they say to themselves: *Look at what is going on in those places, and now take a look at where we live—nothing has happened here, this place is still a disaster.*

The country's supreme leader, Kim Jong-un, was educated at private school in Switzerland. It is very unlikely that a guy who is thirty years old and spent his formative years in Europe is going to come back and say, "Boy, I really like this, with no bars, no entertainment, no cars, no nothing."

These men have been exposed to the outside world, and they know what is going on there. And in my view that is why North Korea is about to open up. And when it does, it will be a formidable player on the world stage. The Chinese are already pouring in. Up in the northwest, they are building new bridges connecting the two countries. There are new trade zones up there. So change is happening.

Everywhere we went we could see propaganda posters calling for one country, two systems—which was the prevailing mantra in the late 1990s when Hong Kong went back to China. If the propaganda is to be believed, the country, despite what you read in the United States, is keen for unification. A unified Korea would be an economic powerhouse. The only opponents of such a positive step are the United States and Japan.

If North and South Korea unite, Japan will be faced with a huge new competitor, much more powerful a competitor than South Korea is right now. There will be a country of seventy-five to eighty million people right on the Chinese border, with lots of cheap, disciplined labor and natural resources in the north and lots of capital, expertise, and management capabilities in the south. Such a country would run circles around Japan. The cost of doing business in Japan is high and getting higher. Among other things, the Japanese do not have a lot of cheap labor anymore.

Japan is against unification for obvious reasons. I am not sure why America is against it, other than simple inertia. For American bureaucrats, who are intellectually lethargic, characteristically slow to change their thinking, a divided Korea is a way of life. Several thousand US soldiers are stationed in South Korea—it is something of an industry, and an entire bureaucracy subsists on the industry's continuity.

You can see much the same thinking in the way we cut off Cuba. Somebody had a political reason, however sound or unsound, for doing it at the time, but now there is a host of bureaucrats and lobbyists in Washington whose careers have been built and currently thrive on our economic blockade of the country.

They spend much of their time reminding elected officials of all those Cuban exile voters in Florida—who in reality are the American children and grandchildren of those Cuban exiles and could not care less about the evil Fidel Castro, if they recognize his name at all. And once again America cuts off its nose to spite its face. The Europeans, the Mexicans, the Canadians, and the South Americans are pouring into Cuba, buying up property and making investments, and eventually, when we lift the blockade, those same people will be waiting on the beach for us as we converge on the island, offering to sell us property that has tripled in price.

It is just one more example of our being last to the party—we Americans, who live in the land of the free—because our government has protected us, just as they protect us from North Korea. I am skeptical of American propaganda relative to these "rogue states." It is unrelentingly negative, and the information we receive—if history is any guide—is almost certainly distorted.

Where are the investment opportunities in North Korea? one might ask. I invest in markets, and there is no market there, so I would have to find companies, maybe Chinese or other Asian companies, that would benefit from the opening up of North Korea. I do not know of such companies right now. But North Korea is ripe for factories, hotels, restaurants, pretty much anything at this point. North Korea has nothing—no mobile phones, no Internet. Like Myanmar, the country lacks everything from the most basic goods and services to the highest technology. Yes, Myanmar has the Internet, but very little penetration. Yes, both countries have soap, but not nearly enough. Yes, both countries have electricity, but not nearly enough.

Tourism, I believe, presents investment opportunities in North Korea. There are only twenty-five million North Koreans, so there is not going to be a big boom in their traveling the world, but there is probably going to be a big boom in South Koreans visiting North Korea. There will be a staggering business in marriage, because there is a huge shortage of girls in South Korea. South Korean men can look for wives in Los Angeles or Queens, but the main source of Korean brides is going to be North Korea. The north does not suffer from the demographic problem that plagues the south.

I am dying to find a way to invest in both North Korea and Myanmar. The major changes in these two countries are among the most exciting things I see right now, looking to the future.

Another thing I am extremely bullish on for the next twenty or thirty years is Chinese tourism. The Chinese have not been able to travel for decades, and now they can. It is easy for Chinese citizens to get passports now, and it is easy to get money out of China. I remember when suddenly in the 1980s we in New York started seeing all these Japanese tourists on Madison Avenue. People wondered from where they all came. The Japanese were then traveling in droves. There are 125 million Japanese, but there are 1.3 billion Chinese—over ten times as many—and you will be seeing them all over the globe. And not only will the Chinese see the world, they will tour their own country extensively. Both inside and outside the country, Chinese tourism will explode.

I was recently in a couple of Chinese cities. One of them was Chengdu, the capital of Sichuan Province, home to a world-famous breeding and research center for giant pandas, called the Chengdu Panda Base, where Paige and I took the kids. Eighty percent of the world's giant pandas are found in southwest China's Sichuan Province. The facility attracts a hundred thousand visitors a year. I also visited Changsha, a city of seven million people in south-central China, the capital of Hunan Province. One of the things I noticed was that all the hotels were filled and all the entertainment and cultural attractions were crowded with Chinese tourists.

While driving across China during our Millennium Adventure, at a fair in Lanzhou, Paige and I saw an exhibition of ice carvings from the city of Harbin in the northeast. We had missed the spectacular Harbin International Ice and Snow Sculpture Festival that is held annually there, but we promised ourselves that we would get there someday. We finally attended the festival with the children during Chinese New Year 2012. In subzero temperature, thanks to the cold winter wind out of Siberia, we marveled at the massive sculptures—carvings the size of football fields, full-size buildings and monuments illuminated from within, entire cityscapes constructed of three-foot-thick blocks of crystal clear ice—while Happy took great pleasure in joining the locals as they set off firecrackers in celebration of the holiday. The festival attracts an average of eight hundred thousand visitors annually.

You are going to see a rapid expansion in Chinese/Asian tourism. It is going to be one of the great growth industries of our time.

16

CREATIVE DESTRUCTION

"But now the whole Round Table is dissolved / Which was an image of the mighty world," laments the bold Sir Bedivere, the Round Table's one surviving knight, bidding farewell to the dying King Arthur, in Tennyson's *Idylls of the King*.

To lift the spirits of Bedivere, who must "go forth companionless," the mortally wounded Arthur, placed in the barge that will bear him to Avalon, delivers one of the more memorable lines in English literature when he slowly answers:

"The old order changeth, yielding place to new, / And God fulfils himself in many ways, / Lest one good custom should corrupt the world."

Nothing lasts forever, nor should it, Arthur is reminding him, not even a custom as noble as that great assembly of knights.

People who invest in the market are always asking me for

hot tips. The hottest tip I have to offer is to listen to King Arthur. I cannot tell you what to put your money in that will pay off in the near term. Nor would I. The best I can do, and what I have tried to do, is tell you what you can bet on in the coming century. What to expect a hundred years from now is a pretty hot tip, if you view the world, as I do, through a lens whose depth of field is millennial.

The world economy is a system of creative destruction, which Schumpeter pointed to as the "essential fact about capitalism." The new rises and replaces the old. The automobile came along and replaced the horse and buggy. Toyota came along and replaced General Motors. Television came along and a lot of things changed. We no longer sit by the fire at night, reading. It is the way the world works, always has worked, and always will. Countries rise, companies rise, families rise, individuals rise, and at the same time you have others declining. People can try to change it, they can try to abrogate the law of supply and demand, but it never works. Politicians cannot repeal the laws governing creative destruction. Studies show that the bottom 20 percent of society changes every couple of decades, as does the top 20 percent.

Yet they continue to try. You can see it in the simplest manifestations. The downtown area in a given city is seen to be declining, and politicians spend money trying to revive it, only to make matters worse. The city goes deeper into debt. It certainly happened in my town, Demopolis. It happened in Paige's town, Rocky Mount, North Carolina. It has happened all over America. Downtown areas see themselves suffering as modern shopping centers rise nearby, and nobody jumps up with the obvious solution: let it go—tear down all the old buildings and build an up-to-date shopping mall.

People with vision, people who can see fifteen years down the road—who can see, for instance, that *all* shopping is going to be done in shopping malls just across the city line—are ignored. Visionaries are always ridiculed. People refuse to accept the inevitable. (For what it is worth, the opposite is the case in Singapore and China. I am always amazed at how often old buildings are just ripped down. There is a bit of a preservation movement, but creative destruction is the basic rule.)

All empires have ended badly, and the reason is that, as empires, they simply spent too much money. They went into debt, they declined, and they collapsed. Unfortunately, regarding America's decline, I do not see any immediate salvation. After the Second World War, the United States was in its ascendancy, the richest, most powerful nation in the world. We are three generations from our peak. Britain, when headed for disintegration—a loss of its empire, divestiture of its colonies—did not quite understand its predicament until the nation finally hit bottom. And I do not see anything that can save us until we do the same.

The optimists will tell you that America has always been innovative. And that is correct—*has* always been. American students are not urged to study math and science anymore, and in Asia that is still a big emphasis. At this stage of Asia's economic development, that is where the opportunities are. It was a belief in engineering and science that helped Deng Xiaoping lead China to where it is today. Engineers dominated China's post-Mao leadership. Hu Jintao, Wen Jiabao, and Jiang Zemin were all engineers.

Maybe China is not producing the best engineers in the world, but eventually, one has to assume, there will be some great engineers coming out of China with some wonderful innovations. When I was a kid, America was dominant in such fields as automotive engineering and electronics and, well, pretty much everything else, including finance. Today we still dominate things like aviation, but the Chinese are building an aircraft industry, and in twenty or thirty years I am sure they will make us look bad. Finance here is already in decline. Hong Kong already leads in raising money through stock market offerings.

I can think of very few fields in which we predominate today. Microsoft was a wonderful thing, as were Apple and Google, but we do not dominate in digital technology anymore. You go to places like Scandinavia, some of the rest of the world, and you will see how far ahead of us they are in Internet penetration. Apple is currently the most valuable company in the world, but I am not convinced that the next Steve Jobs is going to come out of America.

I see two positive signs of revival on the American horizon, but not even taken together do they lead to a recovery. One is agriculture. As I mentioned in the lecture I gave to Balliol students, I am very optimistic about agriculture moving forward. It will be a lucrative sector of the world economy for the next two or three decades, and not only is America good at it, but in America we have a lot of land. The problem with agriculture in America, as it is everywhere in the world, is water. In the Southwest it is a big problem, as the water table is drying up. It limits the amount of land we can bring into production. But if agriculture prices double, triple, quadruple, as I expect will happen, the United States will benefit.

The only other positive development I see in the future is extraction of shale gas and oil, the natural gas and oil trapped in the strata of rock belowground in the United States. Until now it has been impossible—or extremely expensive—to release the hydrocarbons from the rocks. New technology now makes it possible and practical to do so. Some areas have banned drilling because of the vast amounts of water required and because of the potential for pollution of subsoil and groundwater that hydraulic fracturing, or "fracking," entails. The technology is not great yet. But the studies, if they are accurate, indicate that the United States has a huge amount of shale gas and oil potential. (So do China, Russia, Australia, and a lot of places.) With improvement of the technology, I see extraction of shale gas and oil as contributing somewhat to a slowdown in the nation's decline. In fact, this may be what ends the current bull market in energy someday—all bull markets in energy and commodities have eventually ended—but someday is still several years away, since we are losing all other known oil reserves.

By referring to the nation's decline, I do not mean to suggest that America is going to fall off the face of the earth. I see the nation going the way of Great Britain, Spain, and Portugal, all of which had great empires and inevitably declined, and all of which are still with us. I am not the only one to notice the shift, but I think that in the United States most people do not recognize or acknowledge it, or if they do see it, they do not accept it. I do not like the fact that the United States is in decline. I do not like it at all. I am an American, and a taxpayer, but I cannot live on dreams. I have to live my life on facts.

The United States has been going down this path for a long time. Is it too late to save it? If I were to tell you how our problems *could* be solved, you would say, "Well, it *is* too late."

First, the United States should bring all its troops home from overseas. We should withdraw our military personnel from the more than one hundred countries abroad in which they are stationed. That will save us a lot of money, as well as reduce the number of enemies we make. At the same time, of course, we need to remove ourselves from all the wars we are currently fighting.

I have pointed out the need for litigation reform. Litigation run amok drives up the cost of doing business and impairs the country's ability to compete around the world, in no small part by wreaking havoc with the cost of health care in the United States. We spend 17 percent of our GNP on medical care, twice the worldwide average, and what do we have to show for it? Our life expectancy at birth ranks fiftieth in the world, and forty-eight countries around the globe have a lower infant mortality rate. One place the American medical establishment has managed to cut costs is in the area of hygiene. Hospital infections are now the fourth leading cause of death in the United States—after heart disease, cancer, and stroke—chiefly a result of unsanitary facilities and practices. That is one reason why I have told Paige to get me to Singapore if I get sick.

I have pointed out the abysmal state of American education,

how our children are consistently outperformed by the children of numerous other nations on international tests, even though, along with Switzerland, we pay more per student to educate our children than any other country in the world. Our 75 percent high school graduation rate lags behind that of most developed countries, as do our students' scores in reading, math, and science. It has been reported that 75 percent of Americans between the ages of seventeen and twenty-four are not qualified for military service, in part because they are poorly educated. A third are obese or out of shape; one out of four has no high school diploma, and many of those who do have diplomas fail the AFQT, the Armed Forces Qualification Test, which measures basic verbal and arithmetical skills. Our educational system now poses a national security threat, according to a 2012 report issued by a task force sponsored by the Council on Foreign Relations. It has also been reported that 50 percent of recent college graduates cannot understand a credit card offering or the point of a newspaper editorial. The failure in education is not confined to a single generation. Part of the theory behind free, public education in democratic societies is the maintenance of an intelligent, informed electorate. Our system has been so mismanaged that the very people we, the voters, elect to represent us cannot pass a civics test.

Our federal tax system is an absolute nightmare. If you have a job in the United States, you pay an income tax. If you put the money in the bank, you pay a tax on the interest. If you buy a stock, you pay taxes on your dividends and capital gains. This is money you already paid tax on when you earned it. You pay taxes three times. The implicit deal you make with Social Security is that you put some money aside and you get it back when you retire. But when the government gives it back, the money you have in theory saved, you are required to pay taxes on it. You pay taxes to receive your own money back. If you die, you pay taxes in a very big way. This is money that you accumulated. You worked hard for it and you saved it. You paid taxes on it while you were earning it—and then the government taxes it four or five or six more times.

The successful countries in the world do not tax savings and investment. They encourage their citizens to save and invest. They tax consumption. In America we do the opposite; we encourage consumption. Any interest we pay is tax-deductible. We are encouraged to consume rather than save and invest. We are actually discouraged by the tax code from saving and investing. One of the basic principles of economics is that savings equal investments: $S = I$. It can probably be found in the first chapter of every economics textbook. In order to prosper, we must reverse our priorities.

The tax system has grown so byzantine that Americans, according to the IRS, spend an estimated 6.6 billion hours a year filling out tax forms. The annual cost of compliance to individuals, corporations, and nonprofits, according to various reliable estimates, is between three and four hundred billion dollars. A consumption tax would put an end to all that. You would never have to fill out another tax form—or pay all the lawyers and accountants who grow rich on the absurdity of the current system. And there would be no more black market. A drug dealer buying a

Mercedes would pay a consumption tax. You would eliminate the underground economy.

Change the tax system, change the education system, institute health-care and litigation reform, and bring the troops home . . . is that going to happen? The way the world has evolved, most governments, including our own, are dominated and controlled by special interests. And numerous interests, along with their lobbyists, have become entrenched around the system already in place. None of these changes can happen the way the government works today.

In my book *Investment Biker*, in a couple of sentences, I volunteered what I called a radical proposal: that we prevent our congressmen from going to Washington. Today, thanks to a California woman named Jennifer Ryan, that idea has blossomed into a grassroots movement, Gov at Home. It calls for a requirement that congresspeople and senators work from their home districts and state capitals, respectively, to promote transparency and accountability in government.

In 1789 when the government was established, there were no telephones, the mail was slow, and videoconferencing was unimaginable. So we set up government in one place, Washington, where our representatives could meet. If we were setting up government in 2015, we would probably do it over the Internet. There is no reason for everyone to travel to Washington, especially given what has evolved since the nation was founded, which is a gigantic bureaucracy surrounded and controlled by lobbyists.

When there is vote on Capitol Hill, you see lobbyists lined

up everywhere, keeping an eye on your representative, reminding him or her, "Don't forget about me." Congressional staffers are all wined and dined by lobbyists. Indeed, lobbyists write most of the laws. Constituents have very little input. Nice, simple citizens who get elected to Congress change when they get to Washington.

It has lately become more apparent how corroded, where not downright corrupt, Washington has become. A bill of two thousand pages that nobody but staff and maybe lobbyists have taken the time to read is brought to the floor, and the bill will contain language creating a committee of experts to work out the details. The committee of experts inevitably amounts to a collection of lobbyists with interests vested in the legislation at issue.

This parody of representative government could easily be closed down by prohibiting congresspeople and senators from going to Washington more than maybe a couple of times a year. Rather than travel to Washington from, say, California, a congressman (or congresswoman) would stay home. His kids would attend the same schools as his constituents' kids. He would drive on the same freeways and ride the same public transportation as the people he represents. He would vote on legislation down at the local newspaper office, high school gym, or city hall, where everybody could watch him. Lobbyists could still come to see him, but the same lobbyists would have to go to 535 offices around the country, rather than walk from K Street down to the Capitol, where all 535 representatives are served up like banquet food.

Make them stay at home, make them vote from home, and make them have conferences from home. You can certainly

encrypt anything you need to these days—the Defense Department does it—so security is not an issue. Practically and philo-
sophically the idea is sound, and effecting it would make a huge
difference in the way things are run. Some of these ludicrous
bills, which not even legislators understand, might fail to pass.
Some banker or plumber or schoolteacher would walk into his or
her representative's office and say, "What the hell, do you know
what this bill says? Are you crazy? You can't do this." Just think
of all the travel and housing expenses that could be saved, the
wear and tear on the representatives themselves.

An even more advanced solution that we should explore, as
strange as it might sound the first time you hear it, would be to
select citizens in a controlled, random manner and draft them
into service as House representatives and senators, while still
keeping them at home. Assign them to limited terms of office, as
a form of national service, an exercise of their civic duty. Their
reluctance to serve could be viewed as an asset. Studies have
shown that when people do wind up in positions of responsibility
by surprise or accident or simply by circumstance, they are extremely motivated; they spend a lot of time and energy studying
the issues. There is no better example of this than people who
are picked for juries. As reluctant as they might be to participate,
they serve with no ambition other than to do what is right, and
almost always acquit themselves well. The nation has turned out
many great soldiers, highly motivated and driven, some of whom
became generals, who began their careers as draftees.

The citizen who epitomizes this tradition is Lucius Quinctius
Cincinnatus, the former consul who in 458 B.C. was called from

his farm to serve the Roman Republic, which was under threat of invasion, and who immediately resigned the position of dictator when his task was completed. He did it again in 439 B.C., giving up near-absolute power in favor of the greater good, making his name synonymous with civic virtue. George Washington did the same thing when he declined to occupy the American presidency for more than two terms.

Not everyone, of course, could be counted on to exhibit such outstanding leadership and lack of personal ambition. Naturally, there would be duds. But we have duds now. We have 535 duds. Plus one.

Yes, things can change—but not in my lifetime, nor yours, and not in our children's lifetime, not unless and until we default on our obligations in one way or another. Great Britain, Rome, Egypt, China, the great civilizations of the Western Hemisphere— they were all great once, and none of them, with the exception of China, has returned from decline and collapse to become a leading civilization again. It is possible that the United States will prevail where some others have not. Eventually we will hit bottom, and then maybe in three or four hundred years we will rise to greatness again.

THE REASON I FELL in love with Wall Street in 1964 was my passion to know what was going on in the world, and if I were never to make another investment as long as I lived, I would still be pursuing that passion twenty-four hours a day. That is who I am. When I was a kid, I indulged other passions. I could tell you everything about every baseball player in both the American and

National Leagues. But that is not what I do anymore. Now I could not name a single player in Major League Baseball or the NBA, but I can tell you a lot about North Korea and Myanmar. I am always alert to what is going on in the world. My antennae are always up. Is that spending time on my business or is that just a matter of pursuing my simple passions?

Thirty-five years ago I was sitting all day long reading annual reports, studying trade journals and going over spreadsheets, absorbing all the intricate numbers of various companies. When I was not doing that, I was visiting companies. Now I do very little of that, if any of it. I continue to be alert to the world and keen on it, and, yes, I dig out facts and figures, but doing so is easier today because you can get a lot of what you need over the Internet. I have more experience now, so it is easier for me to make my decisions.

Now an investor can own exchange-traded funds (ETFs). These have been around for only the past twenty years or so, and there are scores of them all over the world. If I decide an emerging market is in a bubble, I do not have to figure out a way to short it. I do not have to figure out which companies, which stocks to short. Now I can short an emerging-market ETF, which is a bundle of emerging markets. I can short an Indian ETF if I want to short India, and the European equivalent if I want to short Europe. I do not have to sit down and dig through the annual reports and assess the management of hundreds of companies. There are a lot of specialized ETFs. You can short oil companies or buy oil companies. I do go as far as to look and see what the funds consist of, and I am sure if I were still willing to dig through hundreds of stocks, I could pick the best six to short, but now I just call up and short the ETF. I am not saying this is better; I am just saying it is a lot easier. And I have grown slothful.

(While ETFs make the world simpler in some ways, they also open opportunities for those willing to scout and research the companies not contained in the ETFs and indexes. There are thousands of companies worldwide with little following because they are not included. An ambitious analyst can have a field day combing through them—with little competition.)

Any spare time I have now I want to devote to my wife and children. I would rather spend time with my daughters than do just about anything else. There is nobody I would rather have dinner with, nobody I would rather do anything with, than Happy, Baby Bee, and Paige.

All my life I had ascribed to the wisdom of Sir Francis Bacon: "He that hath wife and children hath given hostages to fortune; for they are impediments to great enterprises, either of virtue or mischief." I had always felt sorry for my friends who had kids. I had never wanted to have children at all. I thought it was a terrible waste of time and money and energy. I just could not conceive of doing anything like that, perhaps because, as the oldest of five, I had to help with my siblings when I was growing up and saw what a burden children could be.

How wrong I was.

In fact, if anyone reading this has not done it, I urge you to get on with it. Take a day off, if you have to . . . no, do not take a day off, these are hard times . . . take a lunch hour, go home for lunch . . . I have been telling people this since our first daughter was born. And lest you think I am someone who gives advice he is not prepared to follow . . . Paige and I had another.

Happy and Baby Bee are pure ecstasy for me twenty-four hours a day, seven days a week. I cannot get enough of them. I now understand a whole class of people I never understood before: parents. I understand my own parents for the first time. I have discovered emotions I never experienced before. I have wept with joy so many times now, where I had rarely wept about anything before. Just watching Baby Bee run down the hall brings tears to my eyes. They are so much fun. They do such wonderful things. Often, I will look back on a day and realize that I have spent three, four, five hours with the girls. I may wind up going with them to a birthday party. I always go with them to birthday parties. I know that someday I will not be welcome.

I do things with my daughters that I never would have done if I had had kids when I was thirty-two. Back then I spent all day, every day, investing and gearing up to travel the world. My investing now is in my little girls, to make them smart and perceptive. I get to act the part of Socrates passing on wisdom to Plato. I am trying to make sure the girls can make it on their own, rather than trying to make more money to give to them. If I were to double or quadruple my net worth now, fine, but it is just as likely to make things worse for them, to make them useless.

I had friends who competed with me in the races at Oxford and Cambridge for whom the races were pretty much it. They have not done much since, nor have many of my friends from the Ivy League. Some of them had the good sense to inherit money, of course, which has meant that they have never really had to do anything since—other than talk about rowing, talk about The Boat Race, talk about this and that. They have not worked much in their lives. And some of those who have worked have not been very successful. There are 115 agencies of the US government that supervise and regulate various parts of the US economy, and none of the people working in those agencies, including numerous Ivy League graduates, foresaw what was coming in 2007–2008. Nor did many of the highly educated people who work in the industries overseen by those agencies. So I am not sure that sending my kids to Yale or Oxford is going to be the right thing for them. It was right for me because it yanked me out of Alabama, showed me a different world, and gave me a certain amount of confidence. Perhaps for them I will look for scrappier universities, maybe in Asia, where the sense of entitlement is not so pervasive and where few peak at the age of twenty-two. If they want to attend university at all, that is. (Paige's view is to send them to the best schools possible "so they never have to apologize or make excuses.")

I tell the girls all the time we do not have a lot of money. When they are three and four and six, you can get away with that to some extent. But they see where their friends live, and they see where we live. At school everybody tells them they are rich. It is getting harder and harder to tell Happy that we are not. We arrive at the airport, and immediately she asks, "Where is the lounge?," meaning the first-class lounge. She says, "Oh, maybe sometime we can sit in the back, instead of the front of the plane." She is starting to understand. When we arrive at our destination, she asks who is going to meet us; it is customary for me to be greeted by whoever has invited me to speak, and as often as not, by reporters. Her expectations are high, making it harder to prepare her to work for her money.

There is nothing better than having to struggle and make your own way. Once you have money, of course, you do not want to do that. I would hate for my children to have to go out and make the sacrifices I had to make, but at the same time I have to leave them with something more than material wealth. If I can leave them smart, educated, knowledgeable, ambitious, persevering people, I can lose everything and it will not matter—I will have made an investment that will outlive them, a portfolio of much greater value than any amount of money I might bequeath to them; I will have prepared them to make their way without any money from me, and that is much better. Whatever they inherit can be lost in five years or fifty years, but if I leave them with the proper mind-set, who cares?

If I leave them nothing else, I hope to leave them with the courage to dream, to pursue their passion whatever it might be, to dare to try even if they fail. I want them to understand that the only real failure is not to try, the only improper question the one unasked. If I have been successful as a father, each will, when she is my age, look back over her life with no regrets, and her story will read like a tale out of an Arthurian romance, a quest to stir up adventure, a crusade to cover the territory, to scare up dragons beyond every new mountain, driven by the conviction, the unshakable understanding, that money is the lance, not the grail.

ACKNOWLEDGMENTS

I want to acknowledge my parents: James Beeland Rogers and Ernestine Brewer Rogers. Now that I have children myself, I finally understand my parents after many years of having no clue. My girls have taught me a lot about life, opening my eyes to a whole group of people out there known as parents, about whom I knew nothing for decades. These girls have brought out in me emotions and feelings I did not know I could have. I hope my parents gained half as much from me—they certainly made me who I am.

INDEX

ABOUT THE AUTHOR

JIM ROGERS cofounded the Quantum Fund and retired at age thirty-seven. Since then he has served as a sometime professor of finance at Columbia University's business school, and as a media commentator worldwide. In 2007, he moved his family to Singapore in the belief that the twenty-first century will be the century of Asia. Rogers is the author of *Investment Biker*, *Adventure Capitalist*, *Hot Commodities*, *A Gift to My Children*, and *A Bull in China*.